Playing the Blue Note

Playing the Blue Note

Journeying into Hope

PETER B. PRICE

First published in 2002 by
Darton, Longman and Todd Ltd
1 Spencer Court
140–142 Wandsworth High Street
London SW18 4JJ

ISBN 0–232–52476–9

A catalogue record for this book is available from the British Library.

Designed by Sandie Boccacci
Phototypeset in 10.25/12.25pt Bembo by
Intype London Ltd
Printed and bound in Great Britain by
Page Bros, Norwich, Norfolk

Appreciation …

The genius of jazz music is that it takes what is often familiar, a standard such as 'Things ain't what they used to be', a gospel song, 'Hymn to Freedom', or a Blues number, like Duke Ellington's 'I got it bad – and that ain't good', and turns it into something new, fresh and exciting. In such music there is an essential hopefulness, born of familiarity and inventiveness.

In *Playing the Blue Note* I have been grateful for many familiar influences, notably people and places which have been part of my life for a long time. But the familiar has also been enriched by the new and often serendipitous encounters that remain part of life's page and the music it conveys.

This book is full of people, and I hope all who read it will accept their mention as my very real appreciation of their part in my life and journey of hope. Some in particular made this book happen by virtue of their immediacy to its writing: Eirene and Brian Griffin whose Donegal retreat became mine for a generous five weeks; Mark and Rita Gornik, who hosted us in New York for nearly six weeks. Others contributed by their virtual anonymity: Siobhan, who drove me to Glencolumbkille; Sandra, who served me in a restaurant a few short days after her childhood sweetheart and husband of a few weeks had been drowned; Eleanor, a young peace activist who shared a train ride with me from Boston to New York; and the police officer who must remain nameless who showed us around Ground Zero.

Finally, of course, my appreciation to Daphne Jowit, for her work on the script; to new colleagues Mary Masters and Caroline Turner for picking up the tail ends of this project; and to

Brendan, Helen, Rachel and Sandy from Darton, Longman and Todd, for risking another publication from me.

PETER B. PRICE
Feast of the Transfiguration

Contents

For all friends and acquaintances old and new,
who have taught me to sing
and played the *Blue Note* in my life.

An introduction

This is a book about a pilgrimage of hope. My pilgrimage took place in the aftermath of the events of September 11, 2001, when the twin towers of the World Trade Center in New York were destroyed by terrorists, and the phrase 'Ground Zero' became a part of all our languages. The pilgrimage began in the late autumn of that year in Donegal in the west of Ireland, and ended one cold December evening in the Blue Note Jazz Club in New York City, a few blocks from Ground Zero.

I love jazz. It is a medium of music that has the capacity to liberate, surprise and release in the hearer real joy. I like jazz too because it is dangerous. It cannot be played on its own with any real satisfaction and, because it demands improvisation, it requires not only individuality, but the willingness to be disciplined enough to facilitate the genius of others, and to free them to play inside the pulse and reach deep into people's souls.

Being the medium it is, jazz borders on the possibility of chaos. That is why it is dangerous, but also exciting. I am someone who searches for God in the unusual places, among the ordinary, as well as the extraordinary. I am constantly surprised by joy, even in circumstances where there is only apparent tragedy and loss. Sometimes that joy which springs into hope is found in a single individual, perhaps in a casual encounter on street, railway carriage or airplane. The moment of encounter may be brief, even to the point that no words pass, or names remain unknown.

What makes jazz distinctive is the chord structure into which notes are added or substituted to provide a unique sound, a 'blue note'. As one listens to a great performer, someone like Oscar Peterson playing 'Hymn to Freedom', a jazz number based on a spiritual, there comes with the intricacy of improvisation that moment when the theme is almost lost, and yet in the hands of a master returns to the simplicity of the melody which is ultimately transformed into a moment of sheer joy, by the choice of a single note. This I understand to be the blue note.

Charlotte Bingham, in her novel *The Blue Note,* observes that 'the blue note is the odd note: the one that seems to have a life of its own, and yet comes from nowhere. It cannot exist without the others, though, and needs the conventional notes to show up its oddness, its rarity. Sometimes it sounds a little strange, but it is always there, waiting to happen.'[1] That is how hope often appears too – apparently coming from nowhere, but having a life of its own, often sounding strange, yet always there 'waiting to happen'. Such a note not only carries with it the element of surprise, but makes possible an exquisite moment of elation.

And when I find myself listening and seeking to find hope and joy in God, as I do all too inadequately and infrequently, I find with patience and a certain discipline, both in solitude and the community of others, an elation, new potential, fresh hope – a sort of divine 'blue note'.

Ours is an age in which hope is in short supply. I am talking of that hope which makes genuine change possible, the renewing of relationships, the leaving behind of cynicism, doubt and despair, and makes evident a new order marked by loving, forgiveness and justice. Hope is that for which faith both seeks and works. 'Only faith can guarantee the blessings that we hope for, or prove the existence of realities that are unseen', observes the writer of an ancient letter to Jewish believers in Jesus Christ.[2]

The question for me as I began my journey was, and is, where are the signs of new beginnings, new faith, new hope? This little book seeks to discover hope in events, people, prayer and rereading of Scripture. It is not a book of answers, but of reflections, observations of a journey maker, someone who believes all is not lost, and that God is still – over all, in all, and through all – the One who continues to surprise, offering new chords and notes with which to offer praise.

1

'A three-days' journey into the wilderness'

'Time is the longest distance between two places', observed Tennessee Williams. I began a journey to two places – Ireland and America. It was a journey I had been planning for some time. It would take me from isolation, solitude, stillness and calm, into lack of privacy, the tension of anxiety and fearfulness, as well as to places of despair and hope.

'A transformative journey to a sacred centre'

In a sense every day in life has the potential for being a 'Ground Zero' moment – for all of us face the possibility of life-changing, even cataclysmic events that either threaten, or give possibility to a new shape to our lives. My time-limited journey would offer moments that would be bound by the kind of time of which Tennessee Williams speaks: moments that appear never to end, as well as events occurring in fractions of a second that will impact upon me for ever. Since childhood I have journeyed to many places, and I have discovered in recent years that those travels are my pilgrimage towards faith and hope.

One of the saddest things I ever heard was from Maggie O'Kane, a *Guardian* journalist, whose work I admire and who travels a great deal: 'The journeys continue,' she said, 'but the pilgrimage is over.'[1] Nothing is worse than travelling without a sense of adventure, of new possibilities. A pilgrimage, observed Phil Cousineau, 'is a transformative journey to a sacred centre' or, put less prosaically, 'the object of pilgrimage is not rest and recreation – to get away from it all. To set out on a pilgrimage is to throw down a challenge to everyday life. Nothing matters now but this adventure.'[2]

The first phase of my pilgrimage began in solitude on the west coast of Ireland. It was certainly a 'challenge to everyday life'. I wanted to observe this time as a kind of late 'Lent' – after all it was to begin in October! I decided to follow, though far from slavishly, the Gospel and other readings for Lent, observing at least in some measure the solemnity of that season in the light of the events of '9–11', and rather nearer to home the threats to the Northern Ireland Peace Process, as well as the more hidden sorrows of our world.

'Lent' comes from the Latin word for 'spring', a season marking the ending of winter, of death, of hibernation, and anticipation of new life. In the Christian calendar it is the observation of the forty days that Jesus Christ spent in the desert, or wilderness, seeking to discern his vocation, and to practise trust in God as Creator, Redeemer and Life Giver.

This time in a 'wilderness', if not a 'desert' for me, was to be for reflecting and praying. In some ways it was a seeking for a sense of completion, a time to give fresh clarity to my faith. I wanted to discover something of what it means to believe in God in this new century, and the nature of the faith that humanity might choose to live by, and find hope in. To put it in theological terms, I wanted to observe places of resurrection in our broken and fragmented world. For resurrection provides the very reason for Christianity. And if 'the only reason there is any Christianity is because of the resurrection',[3] then we need to look for signs of it in the day by dayness of our attempts to live faithfully towards God, who by the resurrection 'has recast the possibility of the human understanding of God.'[4]

The ending of Lent is marked by remembrance of the crucifixion of Jesus Christ: the time of the apparent ending of hope – perhaps the ultimate 'Ground Zero' moment. All journeys, all pilgrimages, both involve a sort of dying, and carry the hope of new life. As one who seeks the path, I find I must also *become* the path. When metaphorically we experience the footprint of God upon our lives, we must allow for things to be both taken from us, and given to us. The one who becomes a pilgrim crosses fields, feels the ground, journeying to touch and see. Not for nothing did the medieval pilgrims need a shrine, a relic, some holy thing to kiss or feel.

My two-centred journey would lead me to touch, taste, hear and see the storm-tossed coast of Donegal, the awesome brutality of the ruins of the World Trade Center, the mean-ness of the streets of Sandtown Baltimore, as well as the company of old friends. In each place I hoped to find people living the faith of Jesus Christ so that it speaks to others in ways that offer life, hope and an experience of resurrection. The events of September 11 have left many in the West frightened and confused. But this single trauma is the daily experience of too many in the rest of the world, every day mostly unremarked and unobserved: a thousand silent holocausts. In times of crucifixion even the most secure in faith ask the question: 'What does it mean to hope for a new day, a new dawn – resurrection as a daily, as well as an eschatological possibility?'

Towards the wilderness – 'Good Lord, show me the way'

Wilderness sojourns begin with journeys. When Moses sought to encourage the Hebrew people who were slaves in Egypt, he visited the Pharaoh and asked for leave to 'Let my people go so that they can hold a feast in [God's] honour in the desert.'[5] Later, after some refusals, his request became more specific, asking that they might 'make a three-days' journey into the desert and sacrifice to our God'.[6] It was to take many acts of persuasion before Moses' request was met.

This book is a journal, not in the strictly chronological sense, but it is reflections on a journey, a journey in, and towards, hope. 'Travelling is travail', someone once observed. It is, but it is also full of unexpected surprises and good things. Life is journey, whether we stay in the same place, or are seldom still. Like all journeys, there are arrivals and departures. In my experience departures are seldom easy. Leaving behind the familiar always holds with it a measure of regret, a questioning of one's motives, and yes, even one's sanity!

I packed my things on the day of departure. Somehow it made everything more immediate, focused the mind, and ensured I didn't carry too much. However, this 'desert' experience would require waterproof clothing, warm sweaters and some resources both to read and write. Of course it required good will and a certain degree of sacrifice from my wife Dee, although she would join me at stages on the coming months' journey. Farewells are best done quickly and with an element of humour – and I was assured that the ubiquitous mobile phone would keep us in touch.

For many years now I have had the privilege of a spiritual director who is both a wise counsellor and a good friend. I visited her before making my way to Ireland via the Cairnryan–Larne ferry. I hoped for some guidance on the wisdom of my Lenten strategy and my desire to rediscover the reality of resurrection, not only in my own life, but in that of others too. Knocking on Chris's door some hours later, I was greeted warmly. We talked, and then went out for dinner, and finished the evening watching my film of the moment, the Coen Brothers' production, *O Brother, Where art Thou?*

Movies often provide us with insights into the lives we lead, or offer reflection on the things we believe, and seek to practise. Despite its title, this is not a religious film, based as it is on Homer's *Odyssey*, but nevertheless it provides plenty of food for thought. My favourite scene is of a baptism, partly because it is accompanied by the most amazing singing of a spiritual:

> Oh! brother let's go down, let's go down, come on down;
> Oh! sister let's go down, down to the river to pray.
>
> I went down to the river to pray talking about that good old way,
> And who would wear the starry crown, good Lord show me the way.

The baptism cameo is highly ritualistic: the converts line up in white and move slowly to the rhythm of the hymn towards the minister who is baptising in a river. The story of the film focuses around three escaped convicts, and one of them, on witnessing this sight and hearing the music, plunges into the river, disrupting the well-ordered ritual and demands to be baptised. This action symbolises something of my feeling about the practice of faith today – how easy it is to let it be if not ritualistic, then familiar and comfortable. The breaking of order because something really is desired and thought to be worthwhile is what is exemplified for me in this clip.

Given that Jesus began his journey into the desert after his baptism in the River Jordan, there was something timely about seeing this film again. I wondered for a moment whether Jesus' words, 'Leave it like this for the time being; it is fitting that we should, in this way, do all that uprightness demands',[7] expressed more of a need for him to go through a ritual, or whether he, too, like the penitent convict, was energised through his experience, enabled to find the courage to break up the old order. I think that Jesus was leaving something very significant behind at his baptism, he was 'repenting' of any acceptance of the status quo, where human beings are ruled or directed either by the Church or the state, to the detriment of their full humanity. Baptism has often been likened to dying and rising again. Jesus' act of 'dying' through the waters of baptism, brought him to resurrection with a new model of living out repentance, 'not by feeling bad, but by *thinking different*.'[8] It is through *thinking different* about everyday things like forgiveness, reconciliation, peacemaking, the search for justice and loving one another, that gives to following Jesus an ever-present hope of resurrection in the ordinary, as well as the extraordinary.

Over a late night glass of something strong and warming, and during the following morning's breakfast, we talked of my forthcoming 'Lenten observation'. Chris suggested some initial structure around Ignatian exercises, which I had found helpful in the past, and which she thought might give some shape to my going 'to worship in the desert'. As I prepared to leave, some words appeared out of my morning reflection that were to begin the shaping process. 'Mysticism in its broadest sense' provides 'personal moments of encountering the sacred.'[9]

Towards the wilderness – 'Connecting one's routine with the divine'

Making my way up the M6 and through the Scottish borders and into Galloway, I reflected on what these personal moments of 'encountering the sacred' might mean for me in the coming weeks. I know, as Anthony de Mello has observed, that theology 'is the art of telling stories about the Divine', while mysticism is 'the art of tasting and feeling in your heart the inner meaning of such stories to the point where they transform you.'[10] It is this transformation that I sought in these few precious weeks. I have a real anxiety of the over-personalising of religion, and was concerned lest this wilderness time should become exclusive and self-indulgent. I feared too the kind of incommunicable mysticism that leaves those on the outside of the 'personal moments of encountering the sacred', feeling as if they are somehow excluded. 'In a post modern society', observes Bruce Lescher, 'the seeker easily becomes a consumer rather than a disciple. He or she investigates different practices or traditions to try them on to see if they fit, if they help.'[11]

I see a danger for me here. I am one who enjoys, and is privileged to have, many new experiences in life, in the people I meet, in the circumstances that evolve around much of the activity of my life. I am all too easily a spiritual consumer. In this time away I needed to find models of praying and reflection that would meet my contemporary understanding of who God is, not only for me, but for the world as it is now. I had been tempted to 'ditch' all the usual liturgies and patterns of worship that I am used to and create something new. However, I know myself, and recognise that anything new I come to must emerge from the familiar, either because of some experience of disclosure, or because the other has become unsustainably irrelevant, or meaninglessly empty. To begin with, at least, I would practise better what I most wanted to do in everyday life.

Christian discipleship is about deepening our conversion in

the light of a relationship with God, rather than measuring our practices by what 'works'. Perhaps this is something that our faith has to offer to our increasingly 'sampling' society. But we can only offer it if what we are has integrity, and if it is to have integrity the practice of our faith must be able to be seen in what one friend calls 'the awful dailyness of life'. Spirituality needs to grow out of the story of our lives, the times of joy and pain, success and failure, fidelity and infidelity. It follows then that prayer, meditation and acts of service must become what Lescher calls 'practices [which] sanctify the daily, [and] connect one's routine with the divine.'

During my autumn 'Lent' it was this discipline that must preoccupy me, for it is often in such practices in the routine of life that life-giving, resurrection experiences come. In many ways the journey to Ireland was a routine that we had carried out many times in our lives. Often the encounters and experiences we have had among those who have been pursuing peace in the Province for over thirty years have been truly resurrection events, earth-shattering in the localities where violence and destruction have been all too commonplace. I boarded the *Superstar Express* at Cairnryan with just this hope in my heart, as the next day I was to meet with politicians and others caught up in trying to win an ever so fragile peace.

I have made this crossing many times. It is our way home. Thirty-four years ago after our marriage in St Columba's, Omagh, my wife began her long sojourn away from home and family, and in the intervening years we have returned regularly, in the good times and the bad. This time the crossing was fast, though bumpy. There had been gales in the North Channel, and the captain advised us to stay seated. I did so gladly and snoozed my way to Larne.

Later as I drove into Belfast I picked my way through the urban motorways, casting an eye at the dividing wall of hostility that separates East from West Belfast. I listened attentively to the local news to hear of any trouble spots. At this time of the evening there was little more than the odd traffic hold-up, but as I glanced upwards I saw the omniscient presence of an army spotter helicopter over the Falls Road. I turned towards safer neighbourhoods, and the zany, slightly chaotic, but deeply loving family home of my sister- and brother-in-law. As always there was time for news, and here, as the Irish say, the *craic* is always good. We argue, we debate, everyone around the table has an opinion, and that evening it was about the latest 'threat' to the Good Friday Agreement, signed by all political parties in 1997 to bring an end to thirty years of violence.

Midnight passed and we had talked for several hours. Before retiring I prepared myself for the time I was to spend the next day with politicians, listening to them talk about the current state of the Peace Process. It had become more urgent; the events of 11 September, as well as an ugly local dispute around access to a primary school in the Ardoyne district, a mixed locality of Protestants and Catholics, coloured things. I knew that at least two parties in the new Assembly had links to terrorist organisations, and the mood at Westminster and in Washington was far from sympathetic to such groups. I wondered how this would affect things.

Towards the wilderness – 'The oh! so slow path to peace'

On the day of the memorial service to the victims of the Omagh bomb, which exploded on 15 August 1998, a reception was held in the local leisure centre for relatives of victims, the emergency services, politicians, church leaders and representative guests. It was a remarkable gathering. Here were people who would never have imagined being in the same room together. This bomb had truly been indiscriminatory. During the course of the day, we had talked with many folks, including the leaders of all the political parties, the Prime Minister of the Irish Republic, and the amazing doctors and nurses at the Tyrone County Hospital who had seen that dreadful day through with skill and professionalism.

My involvement with the process of peacemaking began in 1969, when the earliest of the 'Troubles' manifested themselves in the aftermath of the failure of the Civil Rights movement. During occasional contacts with groups working for reconciliation, I became committed in my own small way to working for an end to the strife. As in all such endeavours, I found that initially I had first to deal with the sources of violence in myself, as well as matters of personal reconciliation, about which I have written elsewhere.[12]

As I climbed the steps into Stormont Castle to meet the various political and government representatives, I realised just how much this building represents the bastion of Unionist rule in Northern Ireland. Here parliament for the Province sat until the early 1970s, when direct rule was reinstated by the British Labour government. Urgent business had taken David Trimble, leader of the Assembly and of the Ulster Unionist Party, to Downing Street, and our planned meeting was deputed to his political advisor and another senior member of the party. The talking was frank – complex too, insofar as nothing that seemed obvious was as obvious as it seemed. The Peace Process was facing another crisis, apparently once again over the issue of arms decommissioning. Unionists were feeling it was time to press the issue; equally Sinn Fein, the Republican Party, upon whom pressure had been applied before, was expected to resist. Impasse.

Later that day I met representatives from Sinn Fein, and listened as they put their side, telling me how far they had come, how agreeing to an Assembly meeting in Stormont was almost a 'step too far', but that they had come to value the institutions that were now threatened by the bid to have them expelled, apparently, because of the failure of the IRA to destroy weapons, as distinct from 'putting them beyond use'. Yet as the day progressed I began to sense that 'something big' was in the wind and, though not expressed in so many words, that decommissioning was not far away. Given the IRA graffiti of 'Not an ounce (of semtex), not a bullet', such an action would indeed be a change of heart.

A Protestant loyalist with links to the paramilitaries spoke of the regret that he felt at the turn of events, of the dangers of brinkmanship. A pragmatist rather than perfectionist, he believed that the current state of the Good Friday Agreement was about 'as good as it gets – or is going to get'. As I had sensed earlier in the day, the apparently obvious reality was less obvious, at least to him! He saw much of the present difficulty as being down to 'intra-communal and inter-communal' conflict – the real enemy being not so much the obvious one, but representatives of one's own historic community. As so often in situations of conflict, a process of transference was happening, and the blame for the particular difficulty, whatever it was, was being shifted onto the wrong person or group.

At one level it was a profoundly depressing day. At each meeting I raised the question of the impact of any breakdown in the Assembly on the working-class communities on the front line of conflict in the ghettoes of West and North Belfast. All parties recognised that in such neighbourhoods the people were the prime victims of political intransigence, but all expressed a powerlessness to change things. The decision by local Protestant residents to oppose their Catholic neighbours' children walking up the street to school, a stand-off which had lasted several weeks, was an all too poignant reminder of the effect of political intransigence. There was, however, one hopeful indicator, in that all the parties of whatever persuasion believed there was little desire or energy to go back to the wasted years of what one person called 'that dirty little war'. All perceived the latest crisis as just another hiccup, 'part of the oh! so slow path to peace'.

One can only hope and pray that they are right. The vacuum that is left when the institutions are suspended leaves plenty of room for the extremists, and it is all too easy to forget that the Omagh atrocity took place in just such a moment. Ordinary folk I spoke with, like the taxi driver, my 82–year-old mother-in-law, and other friends, were all fearful of another political hiccup. I remember Mary Grant, founder of Cornerstone Community, speaking in the 1970s of the situation as 'being held somewhere between Good Friday and Easter Day in our lives'. Intuitively I felt it was nearer to Easter Day, but the conflict and baying crowds of Good Friday could still be all too audibly heard.

Earlier in the week I had spoken with my fellow peace activist and former Northern Ireland Labour Party MP, David Bleakley, and I was reminded of his ongoing instruction in such circumstances to live resurrection hope through

Praying Peace
Thinking Peace
Speaking Peace
Acting Peace.

Later that evening as I drove into a weeping wet Omagh and passed the simple memorial to those who had been killed and maimed in August 1998, soldiers manned a checkpoint nearby, and it seemed that once again nothing was more important. No ashes were placed upon my forehead on this 'Ash Wednesday', but it seemed that the sign of the cross was everywhere today: the voices of the victims of violence once again being raised, while the actions of the powerful are somehow impotent.

2

'One whose gently-holding hands ...'

All journeys have their moments of nostalgia. This one was no exception. Crossing the border into the Republic of Ireland and County Donegal, through the pretty little town of Pettigo, I recalled a Sunday afternoon outing from Omagh when Dee and I were in the first flush of our courtship. I heard the voice of my late father-in-law, as he reminded Dee of embarrassing moments when she was learning to drive. I remembered too on the same road beginning a family holiday, when all the brake fluid had drained from my brother-in-law's car at Ederney. After a frustrating day, when the garage owner seemed to do more damage than good to the car, we were offered the use of a beaten-up untaxed old Vauxhall Viva that looked as if it had seen service with a terrorist unit! Ignoring the obvious perils of being stopped by the police, or the car simply not making it, we headed off for our delayed holiday. There was the moment, too, of passing the graveyard where an uncle and aunt who had provided many splendid high teas in their bay-windowed house looking across the harbour in Donegal town, lay buried. Today the once grand house is a Chinese takeaway!

It is recorded that John the Baptist in his desert sojourn ate nothing but 'locusts and wild honey'.[1] Jesus fasted for 'forty days and forty nights' and, say the Gospel writers, 'he was hungry'.[2] I had certainly planned to take myself in hand with my diet and exercise, but neither of the above options seemed an entirely appropriate diet. Before driving the thirty-odd miles to my hideaway, I shopped in the town's supermarket, including in my purchases loo cleaners and detergents. Hardly a problem in the desert!

The drive up Slieve League, Europe's highest sea cliffs, is fun – if a little hairy! Once at the top the visitor is treated, whatever the weather, to a spectacular view of mountains rising from the sea for over two thousand feet, the cry of the birds and the sound of waves sloughing into the caves and coves. The cottage that was to be my home was not as high as this, and I made the little turn off at the hairpin bend that led down to it. The road was as short as it was beautiful. The cottage was simple: whitewashed, with a slate roof nailed on against the winter storms, it had a parlour, a kitchen, a small bathroom, a double bedroom and a small attic room. This was to be my home for five weeks. I gazed about me and took in the view. Through a 'V' shape in the mountains the sea rolled endlessly into the distance in one direction, and I looked across the bay to Ben Bulben mountain, where the poet William Butler Yeats is buried in a grave marked by the inscription 'Cast a cold eye on life, on death . . . horseman pass by'. The afternoon was warm, all was still, the occasional lark sang in the afternoon sun. Out to the west, however, the clouds looked ominous, presaging a storm tonight. I paused for several moments in gratitude of the beauty, splendour and silence of it all.

My absent hosts had left me detailed instructions on fire lighting, turf collecting, and how to use the washing machine! I unpacked and made their house my home for the duration. Upstairs in the loft room I created a small chapel – an 'Upper Room'. Thoughtful friends visiting us a night or two before I left home had given me a candle. I unwrapped it and was amused to find that it was a Christmas candle, containing the first verse of 'Hark, the Herald Angels Sing!' I decided that it was very appropriate, because around the centre were recorded the words in decorated capital letters 'PEACE ON EARTH'. I had committed myself to pray for peace each day, and lighting the candle on each occasion provided the reminder.

The wilderness – 'An upper room . . . prepared'

Leading from the parlour a staircase took the visitor to a warm wooden-floored attic room. I am one of those people who find a visual focus enables prayer and reflection. Besides the 'peace candle' I had brought with me some artefacts to help me create a sacred space. I laid a small table with a cream-coloured pashmina wool woven cloth, which some Indian Christians presented me with during a visit some years ago. Here I placed a small chalice and paten from the Taizé community, given from the estate of my late and good friend Derek Hanscombe, who for many years inspired and nurtured young people in simple acts of worship and devotion as part of the 'Root Groups' training. This programme, initiated in the 1970s by the United Society for the Propagation of the Gospel, encouraged young people living in parishes across the country to share a common life of prayer and social action in a small community for a period of one year. In front of the table I placed my 'Emmaus Cross', acquired at the site of the meeting of the resurrected Jesus and the two disciples who eventually 'recognised him at the breaking of the bread.'[3] Around the table I wrapped a Guatemalan stole, the kind that priests wear when celebrating communion. This came from San Salvador, which I visited in 1988, at a time when El Salvador's people were suffering a régime of terror, and when many Christians experienced martyrdom.

I had chosen a prayer for peace and I laid it before this simple altar:

> O Lord, you came to bring peace, to offer reconciliation, to heal the separation between people, and to show how it is possible for men and women to overcome their differences and to celebrate their unity. You revealed your Father as a Father of all people, a Father without resentments or desires for revenge, a Father who cares for each one of his children with an infinite love and mercy and who does not hesitate to invite them into his own house.
>
> But our world today does not look like a world that

knows your Father. Our nations are torn by chaos, hatred, violence and war. In many places death rules.

O Lord, do not forget the world into which you came to save your children; do not turn your back on your children who desire to live in harmony, but who are constantly entangled in fear, anger, lust, violence, greed, suspicion, jealousy and hunger for power. Bring your peace to this world, a peace we cannot make ourselves. Awaken the consciousness of all peoples and their leaders; raise up men and women who can speak and act for peace, and show us new ways in which hatred can be left behind, wounds can be healed, and unity restored.

O God, come to our assistance. O Lord, make haste to help us.[4]

The chapel prepared, I lit the candle, prayed the prayer, and thanked God for my safe arrival, and sat for what felt like a few precious moments contemplating the beauty of the environment and the freedom that was mine. A little later I bowed my head and passed through the small door onto the stairs and into the flagstone-floored parlour. In the grate a fire had been laid, paper, sticks, turf, or peat. One match provided within a few moments a roaring, warming fire. Soon the evocative tang of burning peat was in my nostrils, and I settled myself comfortably beside the fire. Outside, the sun had gone, and darkness began to cover the hillside. The wind was rising, and the first spatters of rain were hitting the window, while below the sea was beginning to show flecks of white as the waves became bigger. As I closed the only door leading into the house, I drew the night around me, and settled down to enjoy my first taste of solitude.

'. . . As much part of the problem, as the solution'

By morning the first storm had passed. I had been conscious of its force on occasions through the night, as I snuggled deeper into the cosiness of a warm bed. The dawn was breaking, grey and silver light danced on the remaining white-topped waves below. The fire was all but out, though the house was surprising in its warmth. I knelt down, swept the ashes into the fire bucket, and began the ritual of scrunching newspaper, and snapping kindling, then placing these and a few dry pieces of turf into the grate. One match didn't quite do it this time. 'You will find,' said my friends, 'that the turf fire is a lot of work, but therapeutic, we find – bringing it in, and enjoying the fire.'

I ascended the stairway, prepared the table for eucharist, lit the candles and waited in silence. My intention was to divide my time into four or five occasions for prayer and reflection, and to observe at least three of them in any given day. I decided to use the lectionary readings for Lent at my morning celebration of the communion, and the other at evening prayer. For my midday prayers I would dip into Robert Ellsberg's daily reflections on saints, prophets and witnesses for our time,[5] and I was to discover just how relevant so many of them are to the present world situation. Although not formally undertaking the Ignatian Exercises, I nevertheless planned a period of one and a half hours for praying and seeking God, in order that I could discover once again the joy of God's light and grace, and prepare myself to co-operate more fully with him. Finally, I would close my day with the Night Office, using this time in particular to pray for peace, and to look for signs of resurrection hope.

Many people have spoken about what the impact of September 11 would be on the way we live our faith as Christians, and how we would begin to re-interpret it. Of course the first reaction was to practise solidarity with those who had suffered, and a requirement for justice with accountability. I had detected a mood among many people, including journalists, of the dangers of seeking revenge, believing this to be a sure route to victory for the terrorists. Like many others I called for restraint, and had written to all the local Members of Parliament reiterating the hope that they too would seek to influence government to act with such. I became aware, too, that it was all very well saying what 'should not be done', but governments by their very nature have to act, and the right to influence them has to be earned. What real options were there?

In a couple of sermons and seminars I had given I had invited people of faith to ask themselves 'hard questions'. 'Are we not,'

I queried, 'as much part of the problem as the solution?' Has Western Christianity, with its easy embrace of materialism and Western values, not effectively compromised on the more radical demands of gospel living: of seeking justice for the poor; of endeavouring to understand what it means in such times to speak of 'love of enemies'; and perhaps most importantly of realising that our failure to practise 'love for neighbour' of whatever colour, creed, or class, has contributed more than anything else to the present impasse in human relationships?

I was invited to reflect on 'loving one's neighbour' on the BBC's consumer programme *You and Yours*, and I observed that the people of 'the book' faiths, Judaism, Islam and Christianity, all hold 'core values' in common: respect for the sacredness of human life, compassion and justice, the eschewing of violence, a belief in community, and the worship of one God. These core values I suggested needed to be at the heart of all our worship if we are ever to build a world in which God's justice and peace transcend humanity's inhumanity. Seeking both to express solidarity and to call for this common practice to be recognised among us, I wrote to all the rabbis and imams known to me.

It seemed to me then, and indeed now, that for the human story to know 'resurrection' by making a future of justice, love and peace, we have to dedicate ourselves afresh to the task of radicalising our gospel, of dialoguing with people of other faiths and none, and of repenting of our failure to live as Christ would have us live. *Thinking different* is part of the resurrection process, as well as of repentance.

Just how difficult it is for us to *think different* was brought home to me in the conversation I had had with Chris, who spoke of being on holiday in Northumberland when the tragedy on September 11 occurred. Together with her companion they went at 11 a.m. on the following Friday to the nearest village church, where they were the only people present. This time had been identified as an international period of remembrance. To cap it all, the following Sunday she found only a brief comment at the beginning of mass. How often this was repeated of course is impossible to discern, but our over-individualised and indeed over-spiritualised faith so often leaves us little room for tackling the really hard theological and spiritual issues that emerge in times of danger and tragedy.

Of course there is a profoundly spiritual dimension to all of this. Initially it is that of recognising that whatever 'tower and temple fall to dust', as the hymn 'All My Hope on God is Founded' has it, there are Hands which hold the human race. A friend of Chris in Chicago had delivered a homily for the relatives of victims, and had quoted the poem 'Autumn' by Rainer Maria Rilke:

> The leaves are falling, falling as from afar
> as though above were withering farthest gardens;
> they fall with a denying attitude.
>
> And night by night, down into solitude
> the heavy earth falls far from every star.
>
> We are all falling. This 'hand's' falling too –
> all have this falling sickness none withstands.
>
> And yet there's One whose gently-holding hands
> this universal falling can't fall through.[6]

What Rilke captured for me in that moment of time was the primary need to connect with the God who knows the end from the beginning, and who invites our trust even when the powers of destructiveness seem most likely to overwhelm.

That evening I played Karl Jenkins' CD *The Armed Man – A Mass for Peace*,[7] which Chris had given me. It seemed like an omen, and as I read the cover notes, I found myself encouraged by the writer's words: 'It may seem an impossible dream, we may not have begun too well, but the Mass ends with the affirmation from Revelation that change is possible, that sorrow, pain and death can be overcome. *Dona nobis pacem*.' I had dedicated my first morning's eucharist to the concerns for peace, praying as I took the bread and wine that the 'One whose gently-holding hands' would continue to hold the world back from its own destruction.

The mass ended, I broke fast. The morning was brighter now, and I went to the *clampar,* the turf stack, to fill the bag and buckets with peat for the day's fire. Warm it may have been, but the house soon got chill and damp, and the weather was unpredictable. Logs eked out the turf, and much driftwood got blown ashore on the many beaches. That said, I was conscious that I was 'raiding' the fuel pile of my friends, which had been patiently chopped and stacked throughout the summer. For them, certainly, my 'turf fire is a lot of work'. I resolved to find some driftwood while I still had the use of a car and could visit the beaches.

Preparing the examen

I had prepared myself to spend an hour or so in what St Ignatius called the *examen.* Simply, this is a time of reflective prayer based on readings from the Scriptures, and involves three stages or 'moments'. First, there is a time of offering oneself, and all that may happen, to the Lord. This prayer is exercised throughout the day by observing moments when one's spirit has been moved by a deeper awareness of, or insight into, God. In addition, this prayer is informed by the times when the conscience has been pricked, or some struggle within oneself discerned.

The second stage, or 'moment', is seeking to see things from God's perspective, then looking at the ways in which the day has played itself out and seeing if some initiative of God has been discernible. It is a time of thanksgiving, too, for the graces and gifts that God has bestowed, and it leads to praise and adoration.

The final 'moment' lies in reflecting on how one has failed to respond to God – where it has been all too easy to yield to temptation, or to hold on to some grudge or resentment, a refusal to practise love and faith. It is in such a time that one's 'spiritual consciousness' or vulnerability is touched, and a time of repentance, of opening oneself to the possibility of being loved, is begun. This is not as structured as it sounds. The stages or 'moments' are not to be separated from each other – they are integral, and part of an ongoing reflection, which contains those three aspects. Equally, there, in the cottage, I was privileged to have one and a half hours at a time to give to this, but at home it's another story – and two forty-five minute slots would be pushing it!

All that was ahead. At that moment, I found myself a comfortable place to be. From time to time I took a moment to gaze out of the window at the changing colours of the hill opposite. The wind had ceased, and it was still once again. The only noise was of the occasional crackle of the dry sticks in the fire. The fire was bright and warm; the embers of last night provided the stirrings of the new burning. In a sense there was something of a parable here. I had journeyed long days to get here. In that time I had enjoyed the affirmation and companionship of friends and family. I knew that I was loved. Here I was surrounded by peace and tranquility, and at some level at least my soul was ready.

My prayer that day was 'Lord, I want to do your will'. Of course, it remained an open question as to whether, once that will was revealed, I would want to do it or not! One of the important things that St Ignatius taught was that we cannot do anything for God in any meaningful sense unless we start out from a place of knowing that we are loved. Loved, valued and precious to God. Of all the lessons of the spiritual life, this has been the hardest one to learn. And I do not think I am alone. Most of the problems that face us in our churches and religious institutions stem from a failure to understand and accept the depth of love God has for us. Sure, we preach it and teach it; we use the language often enough, but knowing deep within our conscious and unconscious selves this profound truth – well, that's another matter.

'Do not be afraid . . . I have redeemed you'

As I sat there on that first morning, reflecting on the promise and presence of God's love for me, I had not had to struggle to believe it. I had reflected on the words of Isaiah, 'Do not be afraid for I have redeemed you', and from the psalmist, 'Lord, you know when I sit down, when I rise up', and 'if I speed away on the wings of the dawn, if I dwell beyond the ocean, even there your hand will be guiding me . . .'[8] And this was certainly one of the remotest places! All these words had spoken freshly to me that day, and sustained my sense of being loved. Clearly, this was a deeply personal insight; those same words might not speak to another – and had I not come to this place with a sense of well-being, and the encouragement and love of others, perhaps they would not have touched such a deep chord.

When reading the Scripture, one does not have to go far before discovering God speaking tenderly to people who might reasonably expect a tongue-lashing. Hosea, writing about how God loves, describes him as 'leading . . . with human ties, with leading-strings of love.'[9] I used much of the morning to reflect on the people from whom I had experienced fidelity and loving. Dee and our marriage and our family were one such wellspring. Alongside this I placed the different locations of ministry. There were the first fruitings of 'church planting' on a housing estate in the 1970s, the idealism of community, and the painful realities of it. In addition there were friends, loyal and companionable, fun and occasionally screwed up. The 'human ties, with leading-strings of love' have been many and varied.

I have been privileged in the different elements of my vocation as a priest: these have included being vicar of a South London parish; a residentiary Canon of Southwark Cathedral, where I had enormous freedom to explore a peripatetic ministry; General Secretary of an international mission and development agency, with all the opportunities of travel and seeing a world-wide Church – and now as a bishop. When in my teens I was seeking my vocation, like many I had to deal with the vexed question of ambition. A casual glance at my CV indicates great privilege and opportunity – I have every reason to be grateful and know myself loved. Sometimes I wonder, though, if this had not been my lot, and I had been unwillingly stuck in a situation that I did not find life giving, whether I would feel the same. I continue to wonder. What appears to be a digression is quite important. Many years ago I resolved elements of the issue of ambition. That is not to say that I have not got it wrong on many occasions, but I can honestly say that to date I have not coveted any of the posts I have held. In each and all of these I have sensed 'even there your hand . . . guiding me.'[10]

'Enlarge my vision'

A book that I remember with affection from my early Christian experience was J. Oswald Sanders' *Problems of Christian Discipleship.*[11] In it, Sanders addressed the problem of ambition with reference to a then little-known Old Testament character called Jabez.[12] Jabez, one of the tribal leaders, sought God's blessing on his future. Today his prayer has become something of a Christian 'cult' prayer. He prayed, 'Oh! Lord that you would truly bless me; enlarge my vision; that your hand would be with me to keep me from harm that it might not hurt me.' And God granted him what he asked. Naïve as it may seem, that prayer provided a basis for all my praying about doing God's will. I have enjoyed my vision being 'enlarged'. That does not mean that it has been without pain, suffering and failure; and ultimately in Christian leadership it is fidelity, rather than success, that reveals work well done. There have been many times when things have gone wrong, and some words of Paul Tournier often come to mind when they do, 'out of the accumulated ruins some [further] purpose of God has to be found.'[13]

I am not a great 'not my will but yours' person. I don't think God wants us to leave everything to him, so that we become unaccountable. Prayer and decision-making ought to be informed by asking, and answering, real questions: What attracts me to this opportunity? What needs would it meet in me? What would I bring to it? What gifts and experience? Why might God be calling me here? When at times of opportunity or ambition I have addressed such questions, I believe it has led, whether it was wanted or not, to seeing God's purpose.

Outside the rain was falling, and the wind was rising. It would have been good to have stayed in and snuggled up with a good book in front of the fire, but I had promises to keep. I promised myself, and my wife (!), that I would take vigorous exercise every day. The following week, when she would take the car from me, this was going to be essential if I were not to starve! It was a mile and half to the nearest shop. With some reluctance I left the warm parlour and headed up the path towards the Cliffs of Bunglass. The rain was coming down in stair-rods, as we used to say, flowing down the hill in torrents, creating endless rivulets and streams. The way was steep, and I was soon recognising how unfit I was, but it was a good test for the wet weather gear I had bought. It would have taken a miracle not to get wet – the waterproof pants and anorak did pretty well – but I needed the warm bath and the re-made fire to sort me out. And then, as so often happens in these parts, the sun came out to give a dazzling display just before sunset, though the clouds on the horizon indicated a coming storm.

3

Pleasing God . . .

The gale that began blowing the previous night was still strong. I read Psalm 104 in the morning as I began my *examen* time. This psalm led into some reflection about how spiritual freedom grows from being seized with the sense of the love of God, particularly as it is expressed in the majesty of creation; and how all the desires of one's own heart are directed to God, Creator, Word and Holy Spirit, because of that sense of joy and affection.

The day before, the walk in the rain, with the sheer quantities of water pouring from the sky and mountains, gave fresh imagery to the words, 'In the ravines you opened up springs, running down between the mountains, supplying water for all the wild beasts' (v. 10) – though looking at the scattered groups of bedraggled sheep I imagined them saying, 'Slightly overdid it on the rain there, God!'

I headed off in the late morning to Muckros Head, a stunningly beautiful promontory where the waves come in from the Atlantic. The sun shone and the wind blew, and my soul sang as I gazed in awe at the dancing light upon the thunderous, crashing waves. The hills beyond were bathed in bright colours, browns, yellows, greens, while the red and grey in the cliffs was slashed every now and then by the brilliance of uncontaminated sea moss, together with the jet black of gabbro rock. And above all the spectrum of foaming white, green, grey and blues of the sea.

I made my way to the expanse of rocks, flat plains that rise in tiers from the water's edge. Great walls of water towered above me – crashing in bomb-bursts while the strong gale tore spindrift from the breaking tops, forming intricate sculptures of spray, whirling ghost-like, before vanishing into the wind. God at play, I thought – and having a great time.

Making for the sanctuary of Killybegs – 'Ireland's Premier Fishing Port', announce the road signs at the town boundary – was a large trawler ploughing her way through the mountainous seas before me. 'Then there is the sea,' observes the psalmist, 'there ships pass to and fro . . . Bless the Lord, my soul.'[1]

What pleases God?

Sometimes it takes time away from the ordinary to regain a perspective on God. In wanting God to grow greater, not just in my priorities and relationship, but also in those of the Church and society of which I am a part, I turned to Ash Wednesday's Old Testament reading, which was Isaiah 58. It was a chapter about what 'pleases God'.

I don't like much about the way the Church observes Lent. Too frequently it only requires of people internalised spiritual activity. Now in and of itself, of course, there is nothing wrong with that, and I am the last person to deny the place of the inward spiritual journey. But it may not be enough. Opinion differs over what 'holiness' is – whether it is internalised spiritual activity, or the search for justice: the struggle between 'being' and 'doing'. Such matters tend to be juxtaposed. I believe holiness is in fact some sort of synthesis – a bringing together of both piety and justice.

Isaiah records a debate between God and his people as to the purpose of 'fasting' and 'Sabbath'.[2] God seems to be arguing for a direct correlation between the search for holiness and the search for justice. What he does not seem to appreciate greatly is 'hanging your head like a reed, spreading out sackcloth and ashes', nor indeed 'a day when a person inflicts pain on himself'. The criteria God lays out for a just and holy life include efforts 'to break unjust fetters', 'to undo the thongs of the yoke', 'to let the oppressed go free', and 'sharing food with the hungry' and 'sheltering the homeless poor'. Alongside this there is the call for an inward change of attitude, doing away with 'the clenched fist and malicious words'. Anyone who contributes in this way will be known as 'breach-mender' and 'restorer of streets to be lived in.'[3]

The observation of fasts and seasons like Lent and Advent, far from being individual activities, are essentially communal. It is for others to benefit from our obedience to God's commandments. Imagine the difference for the homeless if we found ways of responding to that particular injunction in Isaiah; or in our housing estates and both urban and rural priority areas if we examined and then acted upon what it might mean for the vulnerable, addicted, sidelined people in our streets 'to break unjust fetters' and 'to undo the thongs of the yoke'. I wonder what sort of world could be re-created if we asked: what breaches need mending within our own relationships, in our churches, neighbourhoods, and in our world? Somehow I sense that at least part of the purpose of 'depriving yourself . . .' is to help 'the hungry . . . the afflicted'.

The Jubilee movements of the past decade or so have done a great deal to re-invent our understanding of Sabbath. Jews, of course, observe *Shabbat* every Friday night from sundown until sundown on Saturday. It is an observation that I for one envy greatly, centred as it is around a communal meal, prayers, worship and twenty-four hours of re-creation. But Sabbath is a bigger concept than simply observance of the seventh day. In the mindset of the founders of Judaism lay a radical vision of jubilee, or restoration. Every seven years land was to be left fallow; but there were also obligations to remit debt, and to offer liberty to so-called 'debt slaves' – people who by virtue of economic hardship had to hire themselves and their families out to landlords or other benefactors. Every seven-times-seven years, that is the fiftieth year, there was an obligation to return land to its rightful owner, to offer freedom to all slaves, whether debt bonded, or trophies of war. The degree to which this radical vision was practised is scarcely recorded, but it provides us with a perspective that makes possible the renewal not only of our own society but, as Jubilee 2000 and Cancel the Debt campaigns are proving, a tool with which to re-engineer the future for the nations suffering most from unrepayable debt – a cause of much suffering and injustice for many of the world's poorest nations.

There is little doubt that the big picture is embraced in Isaiah. Possibly the editors of the text of Isaiah 58 thought that too much emphasis was being placed upon a communal search for justice and feared people would lose their inner perspective. Towards the end of the chapter people are reminded that Sabbath is to be 'delightful', and the day, the year or the jubilee itself, 'honourable', in that God is acknowledged as the source of all that is just, good and righteous.

Of course this is where the synthesis comes. We cannot act communally, becoming 'breach menders' and 'restorers of streets', if we do not have time for inner reflection, for listening, being alone, as well as together in true worship of God. The two need to go together, and I am sure this is why the compilers of the lectionary have placed this pivotal passage at the very beginning of the season.

Companions on the way

I rarely travel anywhere without four companions: the poetry and writings of Rainer Maria Rilke; reproductions of paintings by the contemporary American artist Andrew Wyeth; the observations of the naturalist and writer Barry Lopez; and the spiritual reflections of Henri Nouwen. Between them, this quartet help provide companionship, keeping me alert to many of the dimensions of my life journey. I was introduced to Rilke through the diaries of Etty Hillesum, a young Jewess whose remarkable fortitude in the face of impending death has inspired both my personal faith, and the nature and quality of my praying.[4] She saw in him, as indeed do I, someone who reflected on the natural world and the human condition as places where God's revelation could be known.

Andrew Wyeth is one of America's most successful contemporary artists, depicting through drawings and watercolours primarily almost photographic likenesses in his subjects. I first came across his work during a visit to Washington, DC in 1987. I had spent the morning handing out food to poor people. In the afternoon my hosts had suggested I do the tourist trail, so I set off for the Smithsonian Space and Aeronautical Museum. As

I listened to the recorded voices of commentators detailing the billions of dollars involved in putting one human being into space, my eye was taken to the window, where in the distance I could see Columbia Heights, the place that morning where I had offered postdated supermarket food to Washington's hungry. I was overwhelmed, perhaps because of a sense of the apparent obscenity of it all, or the effects of jet lag. Whatever, I had to leave and eventually found my way across to Washington's National Gallery, where on exhibition was Wyeth's seventeen-year study of his neighbour Helga Torstoff. I was hooked, and I have found through his painting a deeper understanding of humanity.

One wet winter afternoon, my wife brought me home my first book by Barry Lopez.[5] She had bought it on a whim, partly because she liked the cover, a collage of coloured pebbles, but also because the notes on the jacket had made her think this would be my 'thing'. Lopez writes about arctic wildernesses, and the people and animals who populate them, chiefly Eskimos and polar bears. He appeals to the adventurer in me, and has opened up for me the capacity to see things on a seashore, or in some wild place, in a way that no one else has. But Lopez writes too about ordinary things, like hands, and he does so with the same ethical quality that governs his observations about how nature should be treated. Writing of being a teenager, he observes,

> In these early years my hands were frequently folded in prayer. They too collected chicken's eggs, contended with the neat assembly of plastic fighter planes, picked knots from bale twine, clapped chalkboard erasers, took trout off baited hooks, and trenched flower beds . . . These same hands took on new city tasks, struggled more often with coins and with tying the full Windsor knot. Also, now, they pursued a more diligent and precise combing of my hair. And were in anxious anticipation of touching a girl.[6]

What Lopez does for me is to bring me back not only to a spirit of wonderment, but also of the ordinariness, the fragility, the clumsiness, yes, the embarrassment and vulnerability that is all part of both my past and present, and makes it possible to celebrate it all. And it seems to me that if humanity is to find its wholeness, to be healed of its sickness, of its division, then metaphorically speaking we have somehow or other to recover that ordinariness, fragility, clumsiness, and vulnerability, recognising that it exists in all of us, and that there is really only One who is perfect, whole, and yet who mysteriously relies for completeness upon a redeemed humanity.

It was in 1979 that I stumbled across the work of Henri Nouwen, a Dutch Roman Catholic priest, in a series of articles on solitude written in *Sojourners* magazine. Nouwen's writings were to impact upon me greatly over the coming years. It is only perhaps since his death that I have understood why: he somehow managed to convey a hunger and thirst for God, and the formation of a spirituality which came from one who was deeply aware of his own flaws and imperfections, and could risk sharing them with his readers.

At a critical point in my own struggling faith Nouwen opened up not only key passages of the Scripture for me, but also an understanding of solitude and the need for it to provide distance from the immediacy of life's pressures and problems. He too visited Donegal, and like me was struck by its people and its beauty.

Tempted to be relevant, spectacular and powerful

During my celebration of the eucharist that morning, the Gospel passage was Matthew's account of the series of temptations that Jesus faced in the wilderness.[7] Perhaps this might not seem the most obvious place to be looking for a deepening understanding of resurrection. However, if we are in some measure to rethink the nature of the gospel we proclaim in these perilous times, then it is important to see where we might have taken some wrong turnings in the past, and whether new insights present themselves to us, in order to see a different, and possibly better way.

It was Nouwen who helped me to see with fresh eyes the temptations of Christ. It was a wilderness time in my life when reading the Bible seemed to offer little to my growing political and social awareness, particularly as I agonised over Christian witness in a nuclear age. I sought a more relevant faith, and perhaps unwittingly one that was rather more spectacular and powerful. Nouwen's reflections on the temptations in the wilderness exposed me to a Jesus who, faced with the temptation to be relevant, spectacular and powerful, made me face my own temptations.

Like us, Jesus also lived in the shadow of a super-power. Admittedly the weapons of mass destruction, while not being as ultimately lethal as those of today, nevertheless had the same impact upon the most vulnerable and weak, the poor – those whom Jesus witnessed as being hungry. Against such a backdrop, the temptation to be relevant faced by Jesus was very strong: to meet human need, become a one-man 'Bread for the World' – turning stones into bread. Unable to ignore their plight, Jesus nevertheless had to find alternatives that would provide self-empowerment alongside divine intervention.

Relevance was important to Jesus, but he understood its limits. He was aware of the extent to which it provides immediate satisfaction and a degree of commitment from beneficiaries, but once need becomes pressing again, the strategy of relevance will be found wanting. It has always interested me that when Jesus did feed crowds of hungry people, he asked them first what resources they had available. They seemed to be part and parcel of his strategy for changing things. No matter how meagre the resources were – five loaves and two fish on one occasion, seven loaves and four fish on another – in each situation they turned out to be the raw material by which the transformation from need into plenty became possible. Jesus did enable the feeding of the hungry, but there were limits to what he could do in this act of mercy as he sought to implement his wider vision of a renewed, reconciled humanity.

The desire for relevance, and the temptation to the spectacular, and power, are all too prevalent temptations for me. In the mid to late 1970s I was attracted by the growing influence of the charismatic movement within the Church. Right across traditions from Catholic to Evangelical its proponents sought to wake the

Church up to the neglected third Person of the Trinity – the Holy Spirit. People claimed new power, the ability to pray with greater freedom, some even in foreign tongues. Others spoke of healings and even miracles being performed as in Jesus' time. With the movement came a resurgence of new music, hymns and songs that seemed for a while at least to evoke a more personal, powerful faith. As a movement, it has had a profound impact upon the churches, much of it for good.

For me, however, there were times when it seemed to lead some into the temptation to be spectacular. There appeared an obsession with 'signs and wonders' type ministry whereby healings, exorcism, prophecy and tongues seemed to have more credence than obedience to the commandments to love God and neighbour, or the practice of justice. Jesus' healing of the sick was indeed motivated by care for the sufferer, but it had another purpose too. In his time sickness was perceived as being as a result of sin against God, and those who were sick, prior to Jesus' intervention, were discriminated against. Jesus' purpose in healing was as much to challenge the systems that discriminated against and exploited the suffering and sick as it was to heal the individual. I find this both a source of hope and of challenge. In my faith journey, I find all too often I want to see miracles, without recognising that for Jesus at least they were the means to a wider end, not the end in themselves.

By his practice of exorcism, Jesus similarly sought to expose discrimination and oppression. I have found getting underneath the story of the 'demon-possessed' man in the synagogue at Capernaum[8] has helped me to understand this disturbing aspect of Jesus' ministry. 'What do we have in common?' the demon-possessed man asks of Jesus when he listens to the teaching being given. The man himself is caught in the middle. Oppressed by the religious and social mores of the scribes, something in his spirit discerns both freedom and the desire to remain captive. By 'calling out', or exorcising, the power that possesses the man, Jesus declares that he has nothing 'in common' with the oppressing powers of religious leadership under which this man has suffered in the past. By his action, Jesus not only offers liberation to an individual, but wrests 'away from the scribal and priestly class their "authority on earth".'[9]

As with many movements, the charismatic renewal took different directions. Interpretations like the one above led people like me into a more politically and socially committed interpretation of the Spirit's work in our time. For others it led into a more pietistic interpretation of the faith, seeing 'signs and wonders' as being essentially gifts for the people of God within the life of the Church. Neither group has the complete story, and what I observe with interest today is the beginning of a coming together of these streams of interpretation. If this is so, it is an ongoing reminder of God's grace, and ultimately God's sovereignty.

Jesus is powerful, but it is not manipulative, controlling power. He does not use power, like the powerful, to 'win the whole world'.[10] Such strategies, then and now, lose people their own soul. Yet it seems Jesus did make strategic use of power. First, by challenging the status quo of the prevailing authorities and their grip upon ordinary people, as well as the particular discrimination practised against women, children and the sick, Jesus understood the political strategies of the dominant powers that led to poverty, making many hungry and landless. At the same time the prevailing theology of the religious élite branded all illness as the consequence of sin. Such thinking left many stuck on the margins of the community, often doubling their isolation. Jesus' bold invitation to the man with the withered hand to 'Get up and stand in the middle!'[11] was a simple yet effective use of subversive power. His act of healing declared God's power over the powers of the political and religious élite.

'Fire in the soul'

As I contemplate the way of the world from the edge of it, I realise how the account of the temptations speaks today.

Increasingly I feel I belong to a Church that is learning to walk in the wilderness, learning to listen to God. If we are to be other than an 'irrelevance', then my hope is that people can find what they need amongst us, when they most need it. This means a spirituality at the heart of our faith – a self-evident 'fire in our soul'. Vincent Van Gogh once observed:

> There may be a great fire in our soul, yet no one ever comes to warm himself at it, and the passers by only see a wisp of smoke coming through the chimney, and go along their way. Look here, now what must be done? Must one tend the inner fire, have salt in oneself, wait patiently yet with how much impatience for the hour when somebody will come and sit down – maybe to stay? Let him who believes in God wait for the hour that will come sooner or later.[12]

Jesus' desert experience provided the making of the 'inner fire', in order that when his 'hour' came, he had the spiritual resources to meet it. As I made this wilderness journey, increasingly I prayed too for that 'inner fire'.

Having let Nouwen influence my reflection on the temptations, I was delighted on going to sleep to read a highly amusing anecdote about his teaching at a seminar he gave once at Yale University. So many people had come to hear him that sound-only halls had to be provided to cope with the overflow. Because of his thick Dutch accent and a minor speech impediment, words like 'faith' could sound like 'face'. This, together with

> the university's dysfunctional relay equipment, led to a situation worthy of the circus. He spoke about Christ's temptations in the wilderness – the temptations to be relevant, spectacular and powerful; but when he came to the section about relevance, the listeners in the overflow hall thought he was talking about the "temptation to be an elephant". They weren't so much amused as intrigued – many came up to him afterwards to point out that, although they had never thought about temptation in elephantine terms before, now that he had mentioned it, they could see how it would involve spiritual inflation of the ego. They commented on the colourful originality. Nouwen had no idea what they were talking about but, once the confusion was unravelled, he found the episode hilarious.[13]

Confessing our 'tackiness'

After church on Sunday, the weather was as warm and placid as on Saturday it had been stormy, and I walked the cliffs above Glencolumbkille. I stopped to take pictures and sketch a little. Although it was mid-afternoon and I had nothing to eat or drink since breakfast, I did not feel hungry. Whether it was one of those moments that Jesus is recorded as having in John's Gospel, where he said he had 'food to eat that you do not know about',[14] I don't know. But this was a sacred and a holy place. Here Columba walked, and wherever you go there are *turas*, or pilgrimage stations, where once a year, on 9 June, devout people walk barefoot and pray around the various sites. In St Columba's Chapel is a rock bed, and it is said that if you lie in it, and you suffer from any ailment, by turning over three times and praying in the name of the Father, Son and Holy Spirit, you will be cured. I tried it once some years ago when I was feeling sick – and sure enough I got better!

I came down from the cliffs by the site of St Columba's well. It is a spring, and surrounded by a half-moon-shaped circle of stones. One has to stoop down to the well itself, which is surrounded by a stone arch; to the right is a modern, ugly statue of the saint. Around the shrine itself are rosary beads, coins, a toy car, bits of money and other general tackiness. It is hard at first not to be put off by such things. But as I contemplated these tokens, and reflected on the devotion of those pilgrims who come here, the tackiness of it all fell into place. After all, most of us bring a fair amount of rubbish into our worship of God, not only by what we do and say, but also because of what we are in ourselves. Here I signed myself with the sign of the cross with holy water of the well, confessed my own 'tackiness', and prayed once again for peace.

Before ascending to my 'chapel' for evening prayer I walked out into the brilliant sunshine. Up on the hill opposite, a shepherd was corralling his sheep, bringing them from the top to a lower pasture. His dog obediently sleuthed the sheep into their intended path, and then returned to his master. Together they set off round the rocky headland above the sea to search for the remainder. As I opened the New Testament passage set for the evening, it came as no great surprise that it was Jesus' story of the shepherd[15] who having successfully rounded up the majority of his flock, went searching for the lost ones. For me the moment was a God-given gift, as well as an ongoing parable of the Church's task.

4

'Freely cease from fighting'

'Where are you, God?'

The bombing of Afghanistan had begun the previous evening. I had heard the news at ten o'clock. The first depressingly familiar fuzzy pictures of air strikes covered the television screen. Before saying night prayers, I walked outside for a few moments. The air was still and warm, and the sky clear, stars shining in the deep blackness, and a rising moon peeked over the mountain. All I could hear was the sound of a brook trickling down the nearby valley. I was overcome with the immensity of the peace of it all, and I reflected that these same stars and moon shone over the terror currently raining out of the skies a few thousand miles away.

I ascended to my 'chapel', asking for the first time in a long while, 'Where are you, God?' As long as the apparently inevitable strikes had been restrained, it had been possible to believe that something new and creative in human relationships might just be worked out, and that we could deal with one kind of injustice in other ways than by the response of more destruction and death. Millions of prayers had been uttered for just this possibility, and now hopes were dashed.

I turned, as is my practice in the evenings, to my book of saints and other good people. That night it was the Quaker, John Woolman (1720–72). I was not hopeful about him speaking anything to the current situation, he who knew nothing about

Cruise missiles, B52s or Osama Bin Laden. Woolman lived much of his life in upstate New York. He was a strong opponent of slavery and very critical of his fellow Quakers who were slave owners, and refused hospitality from any who ignored his pleas that they should cease from this practice.

'. . . free that Spirit in which the Redeemer gave his life for us'

The American War of Independence was newly over, and besides the issue of slavery there was also the conflict between the new settlers' desire for land and the Native American, or Indian, land rights. Woolman observed that 'it requires great self-denial and resignation of ourselves to God to attain that state where we can freely cease from fighting. Whoever rightly attains to it, does to some degree free that Spirit in which the Redeemer gave his life for us.' In practical defence of his position he refused to pay war tax and was fined for disobedience. Robert Ellsberg says of him,

> He was determined not simply to avoid all direct oppression of his fellow humans, but to root out any direct enjoyment of exploited labour. In his *Plea for the Poor*, he wrote, "May we look upon our treasures and the furniture of our houses and the garments in which we array ourselves and try whether the seeds of war have any nourishment in these our possessions, or not."[1]

Woolman felt compelled to make peacemaking trips to Indian territory. Of this he wrote 'that I might feel and understand their life and the spirit they live in, if haply I might receive some instruction from them, or they in any degree helped forward by my leadings of Truth among them.' Here was someone who practised what he preached that 'conduct is more becoming than language.'

As I reflected on the events of the night, and this serendipitous encounter with John Woolman, it seemed to me that this voice from the past was saying something important about how Christians should conduct themselves today. Woolman showed me that the decision to choose to 'freely cease from fighting' does not negate the need for justice and accountability. Such a route, however, requires 'great self-denial and resignation of ourselves to God.' But if, as so often happens, God's name is called in evidence of support for military action, as it has been, do we not have some real responsibility to seek to 'free that Spirit in which the Redeemer gave his life for us . . .' before too enthusiastically embracing the god of battles?

In the mindset of post-independence America the Native American had been demonised to the point of being 'enemy to be destroyed'. Woolman's decision to go and 'feel and understand their life and the spirit they live in' was profoundly courageous, exposing him both to ridicule, and the real possibility of misunderstanding and death from his putative hosts. In 1998, I made a visit to Iraq. In part it was to witness the impact of sanctions and that in some small way we 'might feel and understand their life and the spirit they live in'. We found the élite alive, well and prospering. However, when we met with ordinary citizens, and witnessed the suffering and privations they experienced, as well as being beneficiaries of immense hospitality, particularly from our brother and sister Christians, we discovered for ourselves the importance of such actions.

'All nations . . . assembled'

I had kept a late watch the previous night, and as I opened the morning's Gospel found to my surprise that it was Matthew's account of the Last Judgement.[2] For many years I had read this passage as an account of individual judgement, requiring of me that I act justly in terms of people who are hungry, homeless, in prison unjustly, or sick. No doubt such an interpretation did my soul no serious harm. But I have discovered that the key to this passage lies in the opening words, 'When the Son of man comes in his glory, escorted by all the angels, then he will take his seat on his throne of glory. *All nations will be assembled before him* and he will separate people from one another . . .'[3] Some years ago Raymond McAfee Brown[4] pointed out to me that this judgement is on the nations. Here the Son of man will determine which of the nations have acted justly towards the most vulnerable of their peoples. In Jewish thought, angels are representatives of the nations of the earth in heaven – and they carry the story, bearing witness to the activities of those they represent. It is as if they 'tell' God how nations have treated the homeless, sick, prisoners, refugees, asylum seekers and those of other faiths and cultures present in the dominant culture. On the basis of what God hears of the nations, judgement is made. It is a powerful and disturbing picture, but also one that ultimately comforts me.

In the silence of the night prayer, and in the early morning eucharist, I found the prompting of God in both the story of John Woolman, and the reflection on the Gospel. As to prayer, I figured: is not God indeed the initiator of prayer in the first place? And if the overcoming of evil could simply be achieved by praying, what is the significance of the cross? Ours is a world that is held somewhere between Good Friday and Easter Day. It was for me a time of faith. Could I believe once again that the Powers had been defeated by the cross, and that God had conquered death by rising again in the person of Jesus Christ? Yes, I could, but I needed to acknowledge that the *coup de grâce* of visible victory was yet to be revealed.

'Caesar is Lord'

In the morning eucharist, the observation was of the feast of St Polycarp. Polycarp died at the age of eighty-six in the year 155 CE. Commanded by the Roman authorities on pain of death to pronounce 'Caesar is Lord', and to curse Christ, Polycarp refused. 'Eighty-six years have I served him and he never did me any wrong – how can I blaspheme my king who saved me?' he is reputed to have declared. Many myths surround Polycarp.[5] The witnesses of his burning describe 'the fire made [into] the shape of a vaulted chamber like a ship's sail filled by the wind, and made a wall around the body of the martyr. And he was in the midst not as burning flesh, but as bread baking, or as gold and silver refined in the furnace.' Because he did not appear to be dying naturally, one of the executioners drew his sword, stabbing him in the heart, and it is said that the quantity of blood that flowed from his body put the fire out.

We need myths and legends within our faith, even if in time we discover them to be in part at least capable of other explanations. One question that has been around for me for some years in the light of our increasingly conflict-riven world is, what does it mean to be challenged to declare 'Caesar is Lord' today? Caesar represented the political, military and economic matrix that sought to keep the world under the control of Rome and its religion and ideology. Who or what represents 'Caesar' today? Is it the global market economy, backed by the philosophy, the religion, of monetarism and untrammelled materialism, as well as the military and political hegemony of Western idealism?

François Mauriac, novelist and Nobel Laureate, believed that the inner spiritual life ought to connect with our responsibilities as citizens, and reflected, 'Our hidden life in Christ ought to have some bearing on our lives as citizens. We cannot approve publicly in the name of Caesar what the Lord condemns, disapproves, or curses, whether it be failure to honour our word, exploitation of the poor, police torture or regimes of terror.'[6] As I viewed the current state of the world, I wondered if we were being asked, however immediately justifiably in the wake of the events of '9–11', to say 'Caesar is Lord' to whatever view of the world the West chooses to take. Few could doubt that the global economic system through the World Bank and the International Monetary Fund has contributed to, and in part caused the debt crisis. The West's withdrawal from and subsequent disregard for the African continent, together with its relative exploitation of the commodity markets, has left many unrewarded for their labour and investment. While none of this justified the terror unleashed upon the world's population in the microcosm of the World Trade Center, it must raise questions as to why such anger and hatred have been generated.

Imagining 'saving the world'

Sometimes when faced with difficult questions of faith and practice, I find the need for a form of reflection that requires the use of the imaginative and creative right-hand side of the brain, rather than the rational, logical left-hand side. By using one's imagination in reading the Scriptures – something that is integral to Ignatian spirituality – it becomes possible to allow God to speak in other ways. During an Advent retreat last year I spent some time contemplating different passages of Scripture in the light of Rublev's icon of the Trinity. In this icon, Rublev depicts three persons sitting around a table, each intent on the other, and apparently listening to one another. I have been contemplating the grace to enter more completely into companionship with Jesus, and into his mission of saving the world. In the present climate, it somehow seems an imperative.

I read again the story where Abraham was called to leave the economic, political and cultural securities he had known so well, venturing into new territory with the commission to make a new start.[7] He was to be the progenitor of a new humanity, whose example to the world would be marked by dependence on, and fidelity to God, matched by a quality of living in which freedom, justice and mutual sharing of this world's resources would be for the good of all.

It was a bold vision, frequently thwarted by conflict and famine, as well as rivalry and the stockpiling of weapons. How little has changed in our world today! Yet running through it all is the intimacy of a relationship that God had with Abraham, together with a persistence on God's part to see established in the human story a people whose life is marked by right living, of which love of neighbour, just relationships and even love of enemy are to be the hallmarks.

Just how insistent God is about saving the world becomes clear in the story of Abraham entertaining 'three Strangers'. (I use an upper-case 'S', because many believe that the strangers referred to in the account were the personification of the Trinity.[8]) The picture of Rublev's icon came to mind as I began considering the conference between the members of the Trinity as they stood in the shade of the Oak of Mamre – on Abraham's doorstep. We can only imagine what the conversation was about. But as God's overriding concern was both to find a way of fulfilling his covenant promise to Abraham – 'to be your God and the God of your descendants after you'[9] – and of how to save the world, then we may not unreasonably suppose it had to do with the issue of succession. Who will carry it out? There is a big problem. Abraham's wife, Sarah, is passed child-bearing age, and barren. God's 'solution' is the miracle of childbirth, even to one past child-bearing years, and when the news is broken, not surprisingly Sarah laughs at the possibility! God's reaction is not recorded, but perhaps we can dare imagine a twinkle in the eye of the divine, whose heart leapt at the new possibilities for humanity in bringing the promised child to birth!

Externally the political circumstances were not good. The city of Sodom – the Gotham of the then known world – represented the focus of political, economic, cultural and social power, and it was about to implode. Evidence of even a remnant people of God is slim – and Abraham has to intercede with some tenacity to persuade God that such righteous ones as do live there should be spared.[10] I find this story profoundly contemporary, for it touches upon all the issues that face us – not least of which is 'how will God save the world?'

Who is at the table?

Part of my journey to the 'wilderness' was to rediscover something of what it means to pray for and rediscover hope for our time. In reflecting on the Scriptures, and asking the question, 'how will God save the world?' I sought to place myself once again within the conversation that Rublev's icon invites. I asked myself, 'who is at the table?', 'with whom are you sitting at the table?', and 'who is the God who sits with you at the table?' This was a time for the prayer which St Teresa of Avila calls both 'the friendly intercourse and frequent solitary converse with Him who we know loves us.'

During the following twenty-four hours or so the readings had included Jeremiah's encounter with the potter;[11] Nicodemus' clandestine meeting with Jesus;[12] and Jesus' teaching about loving enemies.[13] I sought, in the light of contemporary events, to place myself at the table and 'listen' to the conversations between the

Three-personned God, Jeremiah, Nicodemus and Jesus himself. I was there too and needed also to speak.

Jeremiah observes a potter for whom nothing is going right – his pots come out all wrong. After a few attempts he once again regains his equilibrium and the desired product emerges. A dialogue between God and Jeremiah follows. Over the centuries the vision of God for a covenant people has, like the potter's pots, come out wrong. The nation is 'like clay in the potter's hand'. Jeremiah's dialogue with God reveals a world view in which God, in the midst of international crisis, is a significant player. By his intervention nations are either spared or destroyed. To our modern mind such a view of God is unsophisticated and simplistic. After all, God's love is seen as the very antithesis of such a world view. I reflected that accepting Jeremiah's take on things may be difficult. However, his world view demands that around the 'table' the following question must be asked: 'What is God's involvement in a world situation which continues to permit gross injustice, the oppression of the poorest by the richest, the abandonment of whole continents to AIDS, famine and war?' I asked myself, 'Is there no place for seeing Jeremiah's world view as playing some part in the way things are?'

The 'ultimate insanity'

At the 'table' too is Nicodemus. In a sense he is the moral arbiter of 'good sensible religion'. Well educated, Oxbridge or Harvard equivalent. If he has not witnessed Jesus' direct action against the economic and politically exploitative practices of the Temple,[14] he has certainly heard of it. Perhaps he was even sympathetic, believing as most establishment clergy do that every now and then the institutions need a good shake-up. Surprisingly, given the hostility that Jesus has faced from other 'leaders of the Jews', Nicodemus' admission that the hierarchy 'know[s] that you [Jesus] have come from God' is significant. The somewhat philosophical discussion that follows between Jesus and Nicodemus is, in essence, about the 'ultimate insanity' of God, who unconditionally offers life to his enemies.

Paul Minnear observes of this passage, 'God offers life to his enemies. This is the "ultimate insanity" of the revelation that this narrator [John] is trying to convey to his readers. To believe in that insanity is what requires a rebirth through the Spirit.'[15] Or, to put it another way, by offering life to his enemies, and inviting the followers of Jesus to model such 'ultimate insanity', we discover hope of resurrection in our time.

Around the 'table' Jesus says to Nicodemus that there is an alternative to the way things are; it is the way of 'ultimate insanity'. Turning to Jeremiah, Jesus says that things are now different from the way they have been. God is no less concerned for the political and economic realities that drive much of humanity into suffering, war and violence. But God does not intend salvation to be brought about through the repetition of mimetic violence – 'an eye for an eye, a tooth for a tooth.' Behaviour like this has to be brought to an end if humanity, as well as the planet, is to have a future. There is simply no alternative.

As I listened, I found that Jesus referred back to the history of the people of God by reflecting on the plagues that killed many of the Hebrews in the desert. Here God instructed Moses to set up a carved bronze snake as a sort of talisman to provide healing.[16] Jesus then observed that as the snake was the source of healing, so would he be. Like the serpent on the pole, he too would 'be lifted up' (on the cross) – for a death to end all deaths. With the killing of the 'beloved Son', God effectively allows humanity its ultimate sin, to kill God. If people can grasp this – and this is why the resurrection is so important in Christian faith, because without it God is ultimately defeated – those who believe in the saving activity of Jesus may inherit 'eternal life'.

The 'eternal life' Jesus offers is not primarily about life after death. Rather, it is a life that embraces the eternal qualities of the covenant: true justice, right living, peacemaking. These core values of the Kingdom are what Jesus both announces and exemplifies through his life, death and resurrection. By choosing 'light' over 'darkness', Jesus invites Nicodemus not so much to personal salvation, but to choose freely new attitudes and behaviour as a representative leader of the Jews. And to people like me, whose attitudes are all too often like those of Nicodemus, he offers the same.

The conversation begins to turn towards Jesus himself. 'In the face of all of this,' those 'around the table' ask, 'how do *you* say we should act?' At first Jesus takes the known and acceptable face of religion, 'love your neighbour', but then adds to it three shocking new instructions: 'love your enemies . . . pray for those who persecute you . . . set no bounds to your love.' The saving of the world that began with Abraham and the continuation of a blood line ends with the 'ultimate insanity' of loving enemies. And this 'ultimate insanity' is demonstrated by God in the person of Jesus, who offers up his life for the world, bringing to an end for all time the need for violence as the means by which humanity settles its disputes.

Witnesses to a new fire

The questioners turn to me: 'And you, where do you stand in all this?' It would be easy to say, 'I am with you, Jesus, on this one', but in order to do that I need to know why. To begin with I find it easier to call other witnesses to the 'table', people who have inspired me and whose conviction has to some degree borne witness to mine. I call first Kathë Kollwitz, an artist and a mother who lost her son Peter in the First World War, and in the Second World War her husband and grandson Peter, and who reflected, 'One day, a new idea will arise and there will be an end to all wars. I die convinced of this. It will need much hard work, but it will be achieved.'[17] Her 'new idea' is in fact Jesus' 'old idea', and indeed it incorporates Woolman's 'self-denial and resignation of ourselves to God . . . to free that Spirit in which the Redeemer gave his life for us.'

I call to the 'table' too the veteran peace activist A.J. Muste,[18] who understood that 'Joy and growth come from following our deepest impulses, however foolish they seem to some, or dangerous, and even though the apparent outcome may be defeat. For the way of peace is really a seamless garment that must cover the whole of life and must be applied to all its relationships.' He too echoes the 'ultimate insanity' of God of offering life to enemies.

For these times I suppose that I find myself hoping for the Church to become what John Howard Griffin, author of *Black Like Me*, refers to as an 'Abrahamic minority'. 'The world,' he says, 'has always been saved by an Abrahamic minority. There have always been a few who in times of great trouble become keenly aware of the underlying tragedy: the needless destruction of humanity . . .'[19] That is what I believe we must become if we are to be true witnesses of Jesus Christ.

For churchmen like myself, the temptation is always to play it safe. There is also the moral pressure not to rock the boat. So for me the voice of the founder of the *Catholic Worker* and fearless champion of the poor, Dorothy Day, has to be brought to the 'table'.

> It was after her conversion to Catholicism that Dorothy found the meaning to go on. As a Catholic she put the scripture ahead of the system and the Gospel ahead of the government at all times in a church that itself, her communist friends were quick to point out, had long been the hand-maiden of the government's theology of defence and theology of capitalism and theology of civic religion.[20]

A paradigm shift to more authentic gospel living

By calling such witnesses to the 'table', I believe there is a need for the Church of which I am a part to be committed to a more authentic practice of gospel values. From my place at the table I believe we must live as those who choose the 'ultimate insanity' of loving enemies, without qualifying it through justification of acts of violence, yet at the same time recognising the need for bringing the perpetrators of violence to justice.

At present I am aware that for any move towards more authentic gospel living, there has to be something of a paradigm shift in our understanding of God, and the role of the Church in the world. Such a shift begins by having the courage to expose the anger and sense of injustice that in most cases have been the cause of unspeakable violence in the first place. Woolman's example of not simply avoiding all direct oppression of other human beings, but being willing to root out 'any direct enjoyment of exploited labour' and to see 'whether the seeds of war have any nourishment in these our possessions or not', is a gospel priority. The Jubilee 2000 campaign was one such model of this gospel priority; but the very fact that no significant movement has yet replaced it indicates the difficulty of the challenge. We need to develop a mindset in our spirituality, prayer and lifestyle that reflects a keen awareness of the 'underlying tragedy: the needless destruction of humanity'. Within our churches we must allow cells of people who will represent those 'Abrahamic minorities', and space must be made within the life of those institutions to ensure their voices will be regularly heard.

Finding a willingness to go to those who are perceived as enemy to 'feel and understand their life and the spirit they live in' takes vision and courage, but this gospel 'conduct is more becoming than language.' Above all, we need to practise within our churches putting 'scripture ahead of the system, and the Gospel ahead of the government at all times'. Much as I should like to believe that all are called to this, as so often it usually takes a small determined 'Abrahamic minority' to give these things voice and action. Such people need to be listened to, and the listeners need to learn how to pray for the 'great self-denial and resignation of ourselves to God to attain that state where we can freely cease from fighting.'

As the day ended I was conscious of how much I had been fighting in myself and how much I wanted to do what was 'right'. In some ways I had been trying to justify myself in this new freedom, and despite moments of intimacy I had become aware of working too much out, rather than enjoying the relationship I was rediscovering. I called to mind some words of my spiritual director a few years ago when I confessed to finding relating to God 'hard work': 'If I was building a relationship with someone and they called it "work",' she remarked, 'that would be the end of the relationship!' So in the evening I forwent prayer in chapel, and sat looking into the fire, listening to its sounds, bathing in its warmth, and with a self-indulgent glass of Jameson's, allowed my soul to be warmed.

5

'Watch and pray'

Grieshog – *Protecting the embers*

Keeping the fire in at night was becoming a necessity. After an exceptionally mild spell for the time of year, it was beginning to get colder. There was around these parts a practice known as *grieshog*. Simply, it means taking the hot ash from beneath the grate and spreading it on the remaining burning embers of the evening fire. It is known as covering the fire. In principle, at least, by removing the ash next morning, and adding a few small sticks and pieces of turf, the fire should re-ignite. So far I had achieved keeping the fire in – but not re-igniting it without rather more substantial effort!

In her book *Fire in these Ashes*[1] the spirituality writer, Joan Chittister, observes that this practice of *grieshog* within Christian tradition is the covering up of embers of burning either by a deliberate refusal to accept a particular insight or teaching, or because the state of the Church at the present time is unable to manage a given issue, which at some point in history has been managed differently. I was amused the other night to read of an early third-century pope, Callistus, who allowed priests to marry, and even ordained clergy who had been married two and three times. In addition, much against the church tradition of the day he accepted murderers and adulterers back to communion after contrition and confession.

Sometimes a tradition or practice needs covering or protecting until its vocation is discerned once again to burn brightly and give light to those around. It seems hardly possible that one such tradition that demands to be uncovered the most in our time is that of praying. Jacques Ellul observed some twenty-five years ago, 'We in the churches are caught in a contradiction. On the one hand there is a manifest drying up of private prayer. People read the Bible less, meditate less, and pray individually less and less . . . There is a growing mistrust of liturgies, of collective prayers and rites, a feeling of invalidity in public prayer.'[2] I understand this. There is perhaps a lost art of praying. Maybe it is because we do not perceive it as something that 'works' in our time, or perhaps it is simply too hard for us. Certainly there are things for which we pray all too inadequately. I have searched in vain in the plethora of liturgies with which my Church is now bombarded for some peace rite, and yet our nation has been involved in four major international conflicts during the past twenty years, and significant internal armed conflict for over thirty.

Yet hidden among the ashes were some warm embers, reminding every now and then of a more complete understanding of prayer. As I daily celebrated communion the following words from the eucharistic prayer spoke for me:

> Lord of all life
> help us to work together for that day
> when your kingdom comes
> and justice and mercy will be seen in all the earth.[3]

It seemed to me that these words somehow summed up the necessity of the partnership between God and humanity in bringing a new order to our world, an order marked by love of truth, justice, and peace. I have often wondered what Jesus meant when he remarked, 'when the Son of man comes, will he find any faith on the earth?'[4] I fear that ours is a time in which there is a paucity of faith that strives for justice and mercy to 'be seen in all the earth'. No wonder Jesus said, 'Watch and pray.'[5]

Has God abandoned us?

Could it be, I wondered, that prayer is the only sane activity when everything around us is so discouraging? Is it the very fact of praying when all our motivation is lost, and all seems futile, that actually sustains faith on the earth? I had been encouraged to think so in the previous few days, and Jacques Ellul's observation that 'to pray is to carry oneself towards the future' seemed to be that very energy that sustains the possibility of Jesus discovering faith at the moment of return.

My period of solitude was not easy at times. There were what Julian of Norwich calls 'dark nights of the soul'. Moments when despair and doubt about the possibility of God acting in response to cries to him day and night were my reality. I wondered whether God had abandoned us. For many, ours is an age where God is 'dead'. In the mêlée of materialism, where possessions, image, human reason and achievement are all, where is there room for God? Equally, when political and military power are rampantly exercised without any regard for humanity, how can there possibly be place for God? We have learned to live with the belief that the prevailing Western political and economic world view is 'good', and everything that does not conform to it is 'evil'. We have fulfilled Jesus' prophecy concerning the way of the world: 'You will call good evil, and evil good.'[6]

Perhaps the issue is not so much one of God's abandonment of us, but rather ours of God. When the gates of heaven are like brass, and our cries appear to be unheard, those who find their confidence in God are required to exercise what might only be described as a radically absurd trust. Because humanity has reached a point in its existence where it feels it can do without God, he, who has patiently offered free will throughout history, refuses to impose, even though in reality we are 'pitiably poor, and blind and naked.'[7]

It may have been my innate conservatism that was leading me to conclude that God does not abandon us, but that we seek to out-God God by abandoning any sense of the divine. In recent times, when political spin and the paranoia of control have made the possibility of the discernment of truth impossible, I have been genuinely frightened, and I cannot be alone in that fear. An account in the *Irish Times* of a conversation between a Member of Parliament and the Chief Whip illustrates this: the Member was charged by the Chief Whip of his party with 'appeasement' because he had spoken out against the war. 'War is not a matter of conscience,' he was told. 'Are you seriously saying that blowing up people and killing people is not a moral issue?' he challenged. In our modern world, it so often appears not to be. Denial of the truth about situations does not display moral adulthood – 'humanity come of age', to paraphrase Bonhoeffer – but displays rather our orphanhood from God.

Prayer as combat

The purpose of prayer in a world 'between times' is to intercede and work for a different sort of future. By 'between times' I mean that in a world where God is not acknowledged as being relevant, there is nevertheless a longing for clarity and the 'knowledge of good and evil'.[8] Ellul has helped me here: 'Prayer has the effect of affirming that henceforth this is our way of life, that the history to be made is not economic, not political, not aesthetic, not social, but in all these spheres it is the history of God with [humanity].'[9]

Such a way of looking at prayer requires something of a choice, an act of will. The biggest enemy of prayer is the self that prefers comfort to combat, despair to hope, and disbelief to belief. In my youth I was something of a sprinter. Every now and then some jaundiced PE teacher would tell me I could run and send me on a cross country course, in which invariably I came last; or the same guy would suggest, 'Price, you would make a good hurdler.' Price didn't! But the illustration serves a useful purpose. Prayer requires the kind of gathering together of the self in the way that hurdlers must do in order to get over the obstacles ahead, or long-distance runners before a race. If we want to pray, we have to get ourselves together, and conquer the self that subliminally asks the question: 'What's the use?' As these militaristic overtones suggest, prayer does become an act of combat, first against ourselves and our wimpishness; then against the forces we would see overthrown, and situations changed for good.

It is in the nature of pilgrimage journeys, or retreats such as mine, that insights and even 'answers' to prayer come. A little over a week previously despair had once again entered into the peacemaking process in Northern Ireland. The usual medley of tunes was being played, politicians were resigning, demands were being made, threats of a return to 'direct rule', and the inevitable street violence that accompanies such political vicissitudes followed. For years, people had prayed for 'peace in Ireland'. There had been many false dawns, but many believed that the 'Good Friday Agreement' offered the best hope so far. But it had been a long haul; issues from the de-commissioning of weapons to the changing of cap badges on police uniforms produced intransigence within all parties. For years the most radical of the armed revolutionary movements, the Provisional IRA, had announced in its street hoarding graffiti: 'Not an ounce (of semtex); not a bullet'.

Yet within the previous few days something of a miracle had happened. This most intransigent of revolutionary forces had finally, to the satisfaction of the international commissioner appointed to manage de-commissioning, destroyed part of its arsenal of weapons.

Reconciliation the toughest show in town

People like me who pray for peace often give up at the first hurdle. When human beings reach the kind of *extremis* that causes them to act with apparent callousness and total disregard for human life, as often it seemed that the terrorist campaigns of the past thirty years in Ireland did, it is not unreasonable to see the divide between protagonists as unbridgeable. The Christian faith has at its heart the doctrine and practice of reconciliation. Like peace, we prefer to love the *idea* of reconciliation, rather than *make* it. Jesus said, 'Blessed are the peace*makers*'[10] – not peace *lovers.*

St Paul understood the challenge of all this when he spoke of God's work as being reconciliation, 'not holding anyone's faults against them.'[11] In our domesticated religion we tend to minimise the power of these words, placing them against the kind of domestic sins we almost casually confess on Sundays. We cannot imagine putting into the pot the extremities of violence that filled us with horror as we witnessed them from the comfort of our living rooms. For many engaged at the coalface of the Peace Process in Ireland, such realities have had to be faced. Reconciliation is the toughest show in town. When we pray for peace and ask for God's reconciling activity, we need to do so with a degree of realism for what is actually at stake: a willingness to give up elements of long-held ideals, to accept 'loss of face', and finally to receive the opponent as 'brother' or 'sister', as well as having to deal with the memories of the holocausts that have been enacted.

In the light of this, those who would take on the task of praying have to 'count the cost'. Or, as Ellul has put it, 'genuine prayer is infinitely simple and radically serious: we need to sit down first and count the cost, to see whether we can complete the tower, whether the army at our disposal (Our Father) is sufficient for the battle.'[12] St Paul did not underestimate the task of Christian commitment to reconciliation – 'God was in Christ reconciling the world to himself' – and that took the crucifixion to achieve – and yet, says Paul, God 'is entrusting to us the message of reconciliation.'[13]

I confess that this idea of 'counting the cost' of praying is one that I have neglected to take seriously. This has been a mistake, because it has reduced praying too often to a whim, a good intention, even a duty. Within the 'collective prayers and rites' that form part of the public liturgy Sunday by Sunday are prayers for the civil authorities, for monarchs, presidents, prime ministers, governments and the like. Such people no doubt need, and indeed deserve our prayers. Public office is not easy to undertake these days, and there is often plenty of unfounded cynicism about the motives of those who aspire to political leadership. 'Counting of the cost' of praying requires realism as to what can be achieved by that prayer.

Pray realistically for those in authority

The reason for praying for those 'in authority, [is] so that we may be able to live peaceful and quiet lives.'[14] This is a realistic prayer. We should not expect more than the authorities can deliver. Justice, truth, freedom or answers are not basically the 'stuff' of the powerful. By and large those in authority manage things, and we should ask in God's name of them only what they can deliver: stability and good order, peace, safe streets and the like. It is the task of the people of God to work for justice, to seek truth and pursue it, and to live in a spirit of freedom. It follows that unless such things that make human life physically possible are in place, it becomes more difficult for 'gospel values' to be lived out.

Whenever we face times of conflict and of fear, our need to pray for our world that it may be fit to live in becomes more urgent. Because violence, exploitation and rapaciousness in all its forms threaten the very life of humanity, we are right to pray that the authorities will not only desist from it themselves, but work to halt all who seek to attain their ends by violence and force. 'Total involvement in prayer', reflects Ellul, 'demands of us a participation in society, in the lives of those close to us, of those at a distance, of intimate friends and strangers. Prayer has no limits.'[15] Because prayer and action are co-companions, we need to take care over the issues we commit to prayer.

Finding 'stretcher bearers'

Although much prayer is privately made, praying is not a task to be undertaken exclusively on our own. We need 'stretcher bearers' – people who will help carry us, particularly when we feel discouraged, or paralysed by the sheer impossibility of it all. I was reminded of this idea of 'stretcher bearers' as Dee, my wife, came to join me and I had a break from my solitariness. Some time ago she was advised by a spiritual counsellor to find some 'stretcher bearers' with whom to share the sojourn of faith. The idea comes from the story in the Gospel of Mark where a paralysed man is brought to Jesus,[16] and it works on the principle that there are always people to carry the other. Dee's small group of 'stretcher bearers' meet to share what matters to them, pray for one another and offer support.

I had gone to meet Dee and we were travelling towards a marvellous sandy strand at Rossnowlagh on the Donegal coast. It was here we had spent our first times alone together; here too that we had brought our children, and from here that we had first heard about the outbreaks of violence in Northern Ireland over thirty years before. We walked along the strand against the sound of booming surf. Once again the autumn sun surprised us by its warmth and the wind by its strength and heat. We collected driftwood for the fire, and then Dee proceeded to pick up large shells from the beach. 'Did you know,' she asked, 'that when people went on pilgrimage to Santiago de Compostela the journey was so hard that many did not make it? Those who did picked up shells from the beach, affixing them to the walls of their homes when they returned to show that they had made the pilgrimage.' She reminded me that when her 'stretcher bearers' group meets, they too have a shell that symbolises their pilgrimage, and in it they light a candle.

We took the shells we had gathered at the place where we had begun our journey together many years before to the 'chapel' in the cottage, placing them as symbols of our common journey in God, Creator, Redeemer and Life-giving Spirit. We shared our lives together for a few days, and a little later friends joined us, and we took them to some of the *turas* (from which we take the word 'tour') of St Columba, to the cell where he is reputed to have lived – and all suffering from various maladies, we laid in Columba's bed, praying for the blessing of healing. We visited the deserted village of Port and collected small white round stones from the seashore. These I often give as tokens when taking clergy conferences, reminding people that 'to those who prove victorious' in the struggle of faith Christ gives 'a white stone, with *a new name* written on it, known only to the person who receives it.'[17] Before I had left the diocese, I had promised one of my faithful colleagues I would bring him another stone. I had fulfilled the promise.

'To be submerged into God's peace . . .'

On my own again, I drew the cloak of solitude around me once more. Torn as always, in one sense I welcomed the opportunity to return to the more disciplined times of prayer and reflection, after all that was what I had come here to do. However, the 'rich gift'[18] that is my wife and the companion of my life, who has accompanied me for over thirty-five years, matters to me, and inspires me in my faith journey as well as in the dailyness of things. I missed her.

Thomas Merton, a Trappist monk who spent long periods of his life in a hermitage, welcomed solitude. 'For myself,' he would say, 'I have only one desire, and that is the desire for solitude – to disappear into God, to be submerged into [God's] peace, to be lost in the secret of God's face.'[19] Increasingly I understood this; there was in the experience of being in the wilderness an access to intimacy and prayer with God who knows and loves us that could not be found in company. Perhaps without solitude we cannot truly benefit from the company and communion of others, nor indeed find true 'stretcher-bearers' to carry us when we are paralysed by fear, doubt, and the rawness of the daily struggle to keep faith.

Returning to the rigours of the solitary existence took time, and as usual I overcompensated by trying too hard. I wrote for too long, and late, and I became irritated with myself, not a little depressed, and wondered whether this whole venture was worthwhile, and that perhaps I was kidding myself that it was drawing me closer to God and enabling me to re-engage with my vocation. At a personal level I still needed to 'freely cease from fighting', to trust God and the process in which I was engaged, and to wait patiently for the Lord, seeing in the act of *grieshog* what was to be uncovered and fanned into flame from the embers.

6

'Waging reconciliation'

I was feeling slightly schizophrenic. On the calendar the date read 1 November, All Saints' Day. My pursuit of the Lenten lectionary had left little room for the observance of the current calendar, but because I had somewhat contrarily been reading from Robert Ellsberg's book of *All Saints* on the calendar days of the year rather than on my Lenten days, I had been reminded of this special feast day. I spent a part of the evening watching a documentary on RTE[1] on the life of Rufus Halley, a Columban priest who recently suffered martyrdom in the Philippines.

Ellsberg had commented in his reflection on All Saints' Day that 'there is a path that lies within our individual circumstances, that engages our talents and temperaments, that contends within our own strengths and weaknesses, that responds to the needs of our own neighbours and our own particular moment in history. The feast of All Saints encourages us to create the path by walking in it.' 'Pilgrim, there are no paths, paths are made by walking,' observes Anthony Machado. The path to hope, to resurrection life, is such a path. I had been thinking about this as I recalled the television programme, and Rufus Halley's witness as a modern-day saint and martyr.

Like so many priests and religious of his generation in Ireland, Halley went as a young man to be a missionary priest. Like others too he had found the daily realities of starving children, malnutrition and grinding poverty led him to being evangelised by a gospel with 'a hunger for justice' at its heart. 'We learned,' he said, 'that we didn't know the answers – we went to evangelise, and were ourselves evangelised in the process.'

The path that led to Halley's martyrdom in 2001 began when he became principal of a high school that accepted both Christian and Muslim students. In the evenings, in addition to his school responsibilities, Halley worked in a local store owned by a Muslim, where he was learning a local dialect. His involvement in these twin enterprises was in part his answer to the question he faced as a missionary: 'How do we reach out to people in this situation?' He described his work as 'dialogue', seeking to build bridges across the Muslim–Christian divide. In school he would say to his senior leavers, 'Muslim or Christian, be missionaries for peace wherever you go.' He was a believer that 'God is one' and 'God made us all' and that 'God made us to love one another.'

'What help can I give?'

One day a Muslim student of his was killed in a feud between two elements of an extended family. This factional killing was a serious escalation of the feud that had lasted over many years. Rufus went to visit the family to pay his respects. He admitted that he made the call with a heavy heart, for a Christian boy, also at the school and of the same age as the Muslim, had been murdered by an extreme Muslim group.

During his visit, the family made an unusual and extraordinary request of Halley, 'Will you help us?' The internecine feud had escalated, now threatening others. Rufus was both excited and daunted that he, a Christian, had been asked to help Muslims to sort out their difficulties – it was unheard of! 'What help can I give?' he asked. 'It's up to you,' the family told him.

As Rufus visited the parties he explained to them that in his home country there were similar feuds, but that today people were seeking reconciliation after many years of conflict. Eventually the parties agreed to sit down with a mediator and talk together. Finally the day came when they met to make peace. Both groups were nervous, and lots of cigarettes were smoked. People were afraid that things might go wrong. A copy of the

Koran was placed on a table and covered. The terms of the agreement were stated, and then each elder put his hand to the Koran. The deal was done, and peace was exchanged in the form of an embrace.

Before long people came to Father Rufus and exclaimed, 'Peace has started – the commanders are drinking coffee together!' Three months later the leaders met and said, 'This is the greatest thing that has ever happened.' Rufus described his ministry as one of healing, 'to heal the hurts' between Muslims, as well as between Christians and Muslims, and among Christians. Within weeks of this act of reconciliation, Rufus was killed by unknown assassins. His death was mourned by all sides of the community. Muslims asked that his body be brought to their community so that they could accord it the honour they would pay to a sultan, and to say prayers from the Koran. Such dignity had not been offered to a Christian before, and to all the community he was known as Father Popong, a term of affection and respect.

To bear witness

Rufus Halley was in that tradition of All Saints whose path and individual circumstances led him, at his 'own particular moment of history', to engage his talents and contend with his own strengths and weaknesses in order to respond to the needs of neighbours. He was a witness within the meaning of the original Greek word *marturion*, from which the word 'martyr' is derived. Christian faith has always bidden its adherents to bear witness, almost literally 'to be martyrs'. At times this has been misunderstood, even interpreted as a call from God deliberately, even wilfully, to put oneself in a place or circumstance in which life is lost. Such a literal interpretation is not intended, yet the idea of Christian witness is such that it is meant to be offered in a spirit of willingness to lose one's life for the sake of gospel truth.

Bearing witness to the truth as it is revealed in Jesus Christ is about 'waging reconciliation'.[2] The task of bearing witness is seldom an easy one, neither is it something that should be done out of a sense of duty, or because others seek to force us.

'That which is forced cannot be sincere, and that which is involuntary cannot please Christ', the great Christian humanist Erasmus once observed. He recognised the importance of presenting the ideals of faith, as well as the need to behave charitably, and 'to conduct every argument without losing friends, however deep the controversy.'[3]

Peoples of faith throughout the centuries have struggled to understand what it means to bear witness to God's truth, particularly in the light of atrocities and holocaust. From all faith traditions have come calls for reconciliation, for a radical reappraisal of the values that dominate in our world, for a new order. Equally, voices have been heard from within Christian, Jewish and Muslim communities that express support for war, albeit many such sentiments are uttered with deepest caution. Halley's testimony of recognising a common humanity under God of those who are called to love one another is indeed a powerful one. His willingness to walk where others could not, or would not walk led to the restoration of harmony, of *saleem* – peace. Nevertheless it was a witness that was, as with Jesus his Saviour before him, to cost him his life.

'Waging reconciliation'

In the weeks following September 11 the Bishops of the Episcopal Church of the United States issued a call to 'wage reconciliation'. In it, the bishops acknowledged the shattering events and observed that 'we in the United States now join that company of nations in which ideology disguised as true religion wreaks havoc and sudden death', and recognised that they now joined 'into a new solidarity with those in other parts of the world for whom the evil forces of terrorism are a continuing fear and reality.' The statement offered sympathy and sought to share in the grief of those who lost loved ones in the tragedy, offering prayer for the president and other world leaders, 'that they may be given wisdom and prudence for their deliberations and measured patience in their actions.' Prayer becomes imperative too for the military and their families. 'We also pray,' they continued, 'for our enemies and those who wish us harm; and for all who have injured or offended.'[4]

The bishops recognised and gave thanks for the work of rescue workers, 'and for all those who are reaching out to our Muslim brothers and sisters and others who are rendered vulnerable at this time of fear and recrimination.' All of this was set in the context of the reconciling activity of Christ, through whom 'God was pleased to reconcile to himself all things whether on earth or in heaven, by making peace with the blood of his cross.'[5] The bishops then commented,

> This radical act of peacemaking is nothing less than the right ordering of all things according to God's passionate desire for justness, for the full flourishing of humankind and all creation.
>
> The peace has already been achieved in Christ, but it has yet to be realized in our relationships with one another and the world around us.

By seeing themselves as part of the worldwide Church, the bishops called for all Christians to 'bear one another's burdens across the divides of culture, religion and differing views of the world', and remarked, 'The affluence of nations such as our own stands in stark contrast to other parts of the world wracked by crushing poverty which causes the death of 6000 children in the course of a morning.'

'Self examination and repentance'

The bishops concluded:

> We are called to self examination and repentance: the willingness to change direction, to open our hearts and give room to God's compassion as it seeks to bind up, to heal, and to make all things new and whole. God's project, in which we participate by virtue of our baptism, is the ongoing work of reordering and transforming the patterns of our common life so they may reveal God's justness – not as an abstraction but in bread for the hungry and clothing

> for the naked. The mission of God is to participate in God's work in the world. We claim that mission . . . Let us wage reconciliation. Let us offer our gifts for the carrying out of God's ongoing work of reconciliation, healing and making all things new. To this we pledge ourselves and call our church.

As I read these words, I sensed a rightness about them. They spoke to me of an appropriate level of response, a recognition of the real evil that has befallen people, as well as the need to respond. Here too was a cry for God's 'justness' to be revealed, as well as for humanity to respond through repentance and self-examination. 'Waging reconciliation' does not sit easily with us. Justifying war is somehow easier, offering a more natural response to the world's real evils. Yet reconciliation is our vocation, and 'waging reconciliation' has never been more needful.

The task of witness in public affairs is rarely easy. Because even the most vigilant guardian of the moral high ground is, in the eyes of God at least, as sinful as the vilest of terrorists, there is real danger of hypocrisy in all who would take a stand on whatever cause or 'right'. The peacemakers have no more virtue in and of themselves than the just warriors. What makes the distinction is the desire to put love for God above everything, so that sinfulness gets addressed by forgiveness. Thus for the Christian, and indeed for other 'peoples of the book', the authority upon which they stand demands listening to the Word of God, as it has been expressed throughout the story of faith. Not that this is easy either, for much blood has been spilt over the interpretation of texts. Nevertheless, my experience leads me to try and keep on approaching Scripture afresh from within our present context, with our best wisdom. For myself, I must do this recognising the ever-present potential for arrogance and pride, yet acknowledging that for the sake of our neighbours whom we are commanded to love, we can do nothing less in 'our particular moment in history'.

The healing power of the gospel

Here I have spent many hours both reading and listening to Scripture. A recurring question has been, what does it mean for me, and others, at this point in the human story to 'bear witness'? There is an African saying, 'The one who builds the path cannot make it straight.' I understand this to mean that one person may have a fresh insight or understanding, but it takes the discernment of others to give it credibility and bring it to fulfilment. Bearing witness calls for the commitment to work together.

I had been bearing this in mind as I reflected on accounts of healing in John's Gospel that had turned up in the readings over the previous few days. Each had spoken to me about the responsibility incurred in 'bearing witness'. In each story Jesus called for a response from his hearers – he still does.

In John 4 there is the account of Jesus healing the son of a royal official. On the surface it seems a simple story of the request by a loving father that Jesus would perform a miracle by healing his dying son.[6] But the man's status is significant. As a royal official he is someone who in John's terms represented power – 'the will of man'.[7] At first Jesus appears ambivalent, even irritated at his request. Is the official seeing Jesus only as a miracle worker? Frustrated, Jesus exclaims, 'Unless you see signs and portents you will not believe!'[8] But how like me is the man? I confess that at times I ask myself what is the point in having some power and influence if you cannot use it?

Jesus acts to heal the child out of compassion, not because of the perceived status or power of the official. What the healing demands is a response from the official. How will he react to Jesus? Will he simply tell the story of the miraculous healing to his household, or will he realign their mindset and lifestyle, as well as his own, to that of Jesus himself? John tells us that this man 'and all his household believed.'[9] A significant act of witness.

Was this the first house church? In the economic environment of the time a household could be substantial, comprising not only immediate members of the family, but other kinsfolk, stewards, estate managers, tenant farmers, and slaves. If this was the first 'church' it was not an insignificant testimony. Out of the compassion of Jesus, and his willingness to risk being misunderstood, a community of people was born offering a shared solidarity in the task of witnessing to truth. As I read this story, I received a timely reminder that bearing witness is something done not only with others, but out of a spirit of compassion, even though the temptation to achieve the spectacular in the task of 'waging reconciliation' is ever present.

Bearing witness . . . a task to be shared

It is this imperative of witnessing to truth with others that is so important in our individualistic age. We live in different times, of course, from the royal official who bore witness through his household community. But for me this idea of sharing with other people in the task of 'waging reconciliation' is important. As with prayer and praying we need 'stretcher bearers', companions on the way. Equally, any such testimony should be made out of a lived experience. We need to find others who have walked the same walk and talked the same talk as we have ourselves. If I am to testify to a new order, a new relationship between God and humanity in which barriers that have divided are truly broken down, then my life, and the lives of others I seek to live and share it with, must give practical demonstration to that truth understood.

It is said that if you want something done, you ask a busy person. I am not sure of the efficacy of this, but that it is in practice true is unquestionable! The friends who had been with us for a few days during my wilderness sojourn, are, like many Christians today, people of influence in economic, social and political affairs. At that moment they were 'off' the church. Formerly missionaries, they had returned home and attended church with their young family and found themselves under huge pressure to be busy in the church. It was spoken of as their 'duty', and being dutiful sort of people they did all that was asked. No one, it seemed, recognised the signs of burn out, as well as lack of support, that led them to a point of crisis not only in their own relationship, but also the faith for which they were being asked to give so much. Today they are ambivalent about the church; their own discipleship has become protected by their professionalism at their jobs, and their spirituality has become what they can offer each other in short daily times of prayer.

I felt a deep sadness for these friends and the many like them who no longer feel that they are supported in any way in their bearing of witness. Certainly Jesus offered his contemporaries hard choices in following him, yet he demanded nothing of others that he did not demand of himself. Ours is a world in which many of the deep truths of the Christian gospel are not welcome, particularly among the powerful, for they reflect that 'ultimate insanity' about which Jesus spoke to Nicodemus. To choose life in response to a call to faithfulness is not without cost. But like our friends, too many Christians of my age feel that they have been exploited by the church for little more than its own survival, or dare I say to prop up the ego of some inadequate ministry. Many sense that they are not unwilling to serve God, but that the challenges that the church offers seem puerile against the backdrop of the world in which they are called to live.

Loving requires being 'born from above'

When Jesus spoke to Nicodemus of the 'ultimate insanity' of God as one who unconditionally offers life, even to his enemies, he invited Nicodemus to be 'born from above'.[10] This text in the early days of my search for God was used as an invitation to personal faith in Jesus Christ. At the time I had no great difficulty with that, but I am not sure that such an exegesis gives full value to the text. 'To be born from above', observes David Rensberger, 'means not so much to have a certain experience as to take a certain action, an action with a definite communal and social dimension.'[11]

Nicodemus represented the religious élite whose easy alliance with the politically powerful threatened both the quality and power of the faith they practised. By inviting Nicodemus to give up his status, together with the ideology and compromise associated with it, Jesus called him to a radical new approach towards those excluded by power, wealth and status. Jesus' vision was the uniting of all in a reconciled common humanity. All divisions generated by power, wealth and status that prevented this were anathema to Jesus. Ours is an age in which enormous power, wealth and influence is wielded by a very few. For those of us in the matrix of middle class, it is all too easy to side with the powerful, yet ultimately oppressive, powers that rule our world.

Sitting out at the edge of the world as I was, I had begun to understand the fabled experience of Celtic monks and hermits. They chose to struggle against the great Adversary in places of incredible inhospitality. They did so because they believed they could see the thrall in which the world was held. Here on islands and mountains, through prayer and holy living, they sought to overcome the world and its temptations. From the headland above my cottage, I could see one such holy site on an island a little over a mile from the shore. Further south, some eight miles from the Kerry coast, lay the pinnacled fastness of Skelling Michael. Here the elemental spirits of sea, earth and air combined in particular hostility to provide the material background for what to many was the site of a spiritual conflict – and one which brought martyrdom, as well as suffering and privation.

I wondered about those Celtic saints and martyrs against the backdrop of the Nicodemus story. I found it easier to settle for the more domestic interpretation of personal faith in Jesus as Lord and Saviour, because it neatly avoided me having to examine my attitude and behaviour as a representative of the influential and powerful in our society. To quote St John, I found myself rather more comfortable with those who 'preferred darkness to the light'.[12] What lies before us in terms of witnessing to our faith in Jesus Christ is being prepared to enter into the struggle to be 'born from above' – and this requires an exertion of will. Although we do not know the final outcome of this encounter, I take comfort from the tantalising possibility that Nicodemus did eventually achieve the changes in his life that made him a credible witness to the new relationship with God that Jesus offered.

As I reflected on Rufus Halley, I sensed that he had discovered something of the reality of being 'born from above' into action that was both social and communal. He had discovered too that 'ultimate insanity' of loving enemies, or to put it into the language of the Episcopalian bishops, 'waging reconciliation'. I shared his story with our discomforted Christian friends – a risky enterprise, but they could see the integrity of this witness, recognising in it that which went beyond church maintenance, and much of the puerile activity with which they felt their lives had been wasted over the years.

That night I gazed out across the sea to the regular blinking of the lighthouse on St John's Point, and felt it strangely beckon to new waters for journeying, fraught with danger, and yet wondrously adventurous.

7

'It is better to light a candle . . . than to curse the darkness'

Darkness had fallen early that night. The afternoon had been cloudy and cold, but still. I had lit the fire shortly after lunch, and though full of good intentions for reading had drifted off into a blissfully sleepy uninterrupted Sunday afternoon nap. I awoke to the low murmuring of voices in the chimney. I listened carefully but could make nothing of the conversations that appeared to be taking place between a number of people. Curious, I stepped outside into the gloaming. All was still, save for the crunch of my feet upon the gravel. I looked around me – there were no voices, no people to be seen. I gazed across the field to the remains of the famine cottage below me. I looked up to the hills around. Out to sea clouds threatened wind, but as of now all was quiet. I returned to the fireside and listened once again – the 'voices' were still there. A few minutes later the wind that gathered out at sea hit the gable wall, and in the chimney came a roar, the fire crackled, blowing smoke into the room. The voices went.

My imagination had been stirred. A little over two hundred years ago this remote cottage had been part of a bustling village. In the port a mile or so away the herring industry thrived and was widely reckoned to be the busiest and wealthiest port in the west of Ireland. Here too weaving flourished, and industries such as whisky distilling and sheep farming brought comfortable living to many. In the early seventeenth century the British government sought to colonise the Ulster region of Ireland by its policy of plantation. Here Protestant farmers from the borders of Scotland were given great tracts of land, the native Irish tenant farmers' landlords controlled fishing, and the focus of the regional economy shifted towards London. In a short time this area had become one of the most highly policed regions of the British Empire, the local economy declined, and what had once been legitimate activities, such as whisky making and exportation to Europe, became illegal. High rents, and eventually the potato blight which caused widespread famine in the nineteenth century, led to (often enforced) mass emigration to America and Canada.

My 'voices' in the chimney brought much of this back to me, and I scribbled a poem, 'Murmurings on the first night of winter':

I wake from a blissful
post prandial snooze
before the crimson silver embers
of a winter fire,
and hear murmurings
voices in slow deliberate conversation
echo softly in the chimney.

Outside the sun slips grey and watery
behind the hill,
while across the sea
slivers of refracted light bid chill greeting
to the first night of winter.

All is briefly still, and below me lie
the ruins of a torched famine dwelling.

Murmuring voices still speak
though as I look
no one is there,
nor has been for a century and more.
The rising wind, cold, causes me to shudder
and ply to the fire more wood and peat.

The murmurings cease
What voices these?
Ghosts of communities
long ago warmed around the hearths
of crimson silver embers . . .
on a first winter's night.

During the following days I spent time in the neighbouring village of Glencolumbkille. I have been visiting this place on and off for nearly thirty years, attracted to it in the first instance through hearing the story of a remarkable parish priest, Father James McDyer, who ministered here from 1951–82. He arrived in this isolated poor community where few roads existed, and there was no electricity or running water. Here too emigration was rife. After serving many years as a curate in London, McDyer had witnessed the poor quality of life experienced by many of his fellow emigrant Irish. A conviction slowly grew in McDyer, who believed that if the communities from which people were forced into emigration, largely because of economic circumstances, could provide work and a sense of place, then fewer would end up desolate on London's streets. He set out to build such a community.

Ireland is a land of myths and legends. Many of them are about the birth of Christianity. The townland of Glencolumbkille, literally interpreted, means this is 'the Glen where Columba had his cell'. Columba, or the Irish Colm, means 'dove of the church'. However, Columba was anything but a 'dove'! He was eventually excommunicated to Iona because he fought the High King of Ireland over whether he had the right to make a copy of the 'Psalter of Finian', a hand-written, beautifully illustrated version of the Psalms, produced in the days long before printing presses. The High King judged in favour of Finian, saying, 'To every cow its calf and to every book its copy.' This judgement remains the joy of all authors and the bane of copyright editors!

Stories abound as to how Columba brought Christianity to these parts. The most widely told legend says that St Patrick failed to convert the people of the glen, and that a group of demons set themselves up, raising a fog so that no Christian would find their way there. A little over a hundred years later, Colm, as he was known locally, was preaching in Donegal. The story goes that one day a demon threw a burning stick at one of the saint's assistants, Crearc, and killed him. In fury, as befitted his nature, Colm fired the stick back, and as it hit the ground it began to grow and the demons fled in fear. Colm followed, throwing stones until the demons were pushed back to the sea and drowned.

A more sociological explanation is that in all probability there were a number of pagans living locally and worshipping in the old manner. At some point they came into confrontation with Colm and his followers, and Colm won. We know that Colm was not above taking up arms in other conflicts, and seems to have been a successful warrior. Despite this, he succeeded in becoming, along with St Patrick and St Brigid, one of the three patron saints of Ireland.

It was to this valley and community with this heritage that James McDyer came in 1951. McDyer knew his history, sociology and economics. He understood how the region had been neglected, although this particular region had withstood the famine better than most. He knew people's fears of dependence upon others. Despite the passing years, memories of suffering remained sharp. I remember asking a young woman who guided us around the Folk Village, which stands as permanent memorial to Father McDyer, whether her family had ever had to take food from the 'Famine Pot'. This pot provided broth for the most desperate victims of the famine. The young woman replied, 'No, I'm still an O'Donnell. If we had taken from the pot we would simply be "Donnells". Those who took from the pot also had to become Protestants!' I cannot vouch for the truth of her story, but when I talked it over with people in the village, there was widespread agreement over its authenticity.

For the thirty years in the mid twentieth century, under McDyer's leadership, extraordinary changes took place in Glencolumbkille and the neighbouring villages that made up the parish. Emigration rates declined, local industries were established, along with the Folk Village that tells the history of the region in the dwelling houses and artefacts of the past four centuries. McDyer was concerned to bring about resurrection from a people who had been crucified throughout much of the past couple of centuries by colonisation, the loss of land, fishing rights, famine, emigration, disinvestments and betrayal.

I met McDyer in 1979. He was a rugged individualist and, like Colm, a doughty fighter for his cause. He knew the pain of failure, and the fickleness of people who did not always share his enthusiasm for the projects he initiated. Once he commented, 'If I did not work for God, I would not work for man, for man is the most ungrateful of all God's creatures.' However, to him is credited the phrase, 'It is better to light ten candles and have nine blow out than to curse the darkness.'[1] On his gravestone in the nearby village of Carrick it is written, 'He has gone no farther than to God and God is very near.'

I had come here in some ways to see what was myth about the man, and what remained true about the legendary work that he accomplished, and to discover what, if anything, of his legacy remained. The present parish curate made his home available to me and invited a number of parishioners to come and talk. In turn I visited the *Oideas Gael*, the Irish Culture College, and the Folk Village. In each place I encountered people who loved and respected the man, James McDyer. He had arrived in the community in the aftermath of the Second World War with its privations of rationing, and its continuing lack of basic amenities. Then the church was the focus of the community, and the parish priest had real status and influence, and in those days could do little wrong. In the forties and fifties Glencolumbkille was a parish in terminal decline – many of its villages and hamlets became deserted over the years between the end of the war and the mid fifties. McDyer began to persuade people to give artefacts for the furnishing of the Folk Village. Not all were easily convinced, and one woman remarked, 'Don't talk about it, Father, this history of our hardship, or we'll be shamed.'

Meitheal – *'everyone gives a hand'*

When I asked Liam Cunningham, the Director of the Irish Culture College, how he evaluated McDyer's legacy, he spoke historically. The fifties were the decade in which the social infrastructure of the neighbourhood was the priority. McDyer would battle in person with the government in Dublin to achieve recognition for the 'forgotten West'. All benefited from the coming of electricity, mains water and better roads. In the sixties came the economic resourcing, the forming of knitting co-operatives, and the vegetable-processing plant at Meenaneary, a town land some five miles from the Glen, and of course the Folk Village. In the seventies there were new initiatives: a hotel, holiday village and the transformation of the less than successful vegetable-processing plant into the highly successful fish-processing factory, which today still employs hundreds of local people. In summing up McDyer's 'legacy', everyone observed that the most tangible signs were the parish hall, the Folk Village and the fish factory.

All the local guidebooks describe McDyer's work in terms of 'imaginatively founding local co-operatives to halt the rate of emigration.' It is perhaps understandable that his extraordinary energy and vision – 'He was a great dreamer' – should be rationalised in such a way. Here was someone who for over thirty years had galvanised the people to work with him. The village hall was the first of the projects, and here in the fifties and sixties committees met, and social events such as dramas and dances were held. It was a heady time. One person described it as the *meitheal* effect – 'everyone gives a hand'.

There is little doubt that in the person of James McDyer his faith and practice went hand in hand. 'There are two occasions when I find it easiest to commune with a higher power', he wrote.

> The first is when I lie down in bed awaiting sleep. Then my conversation with Him is at its most intimate when we review the day's work. I find that my conversation falls under two heads: the blame that attaches to me during the

> day for constantly thrusting myself forward without reference to Him, and a constant litany of wants. If there is success, I offer it to Him; if there is disaster or an unfair criticism, I give it as a present from me to Him.

The second occasion of his communing with God was, in his own words, 'When I go away by myself to a lonely, lonely place, but it must be somewhere special to me.'[2]

McDyer was trained for the priesthood in the traditional pattern. Throughout his ministry he would visit the sick, conduct weddings, wakes and funerals, baptise, and practise the daily offices of mass and benediction. People observed 'no meat on Fridays', along with the other disciplines of fasting before mass – even, as one woman told me, if you were a young girl who had to walk five and a half miles to chapel each Sunday before breakfast, as well as on holy days of obligation. McDyer had phenomenal energy. After celebrating mass on a weekday morning he would often drive the nearly two hundred miles to Dublin on inadequate roads, meet with officials, cajoling, shaming and arguing, before returning to the village in time to say benediction in the parish church. His preaching on the Gospel would often make connections with the work going on in the community. But he was not without his critics. One summed up what many felt: 'Sure I don't know what's taking me to mass these days, hearing sermons about carrots and vegetables.'

'Everything is made easy today'

Today Glencolumbkille is, if not affluent, then 'well set', as they say. The church remains a significant feature of contemporary life, but the uncovering of scandals in the wider Church, together with a general lack of respect for people because of their position, has led to a different mood. The Second Vatican Council impacted upon the community in the mid to late sixties when the Latin mass was replaced by the vernacular. From then on, as one of my respondents observed, 'The church bent over backwards to accommodate the people. Everything is made easy today. Only the schools close now for the holy days of obligation.'

Whether that reflection was universally held may be open to question, but undoubtedly, 'the days of eating bread are forgotten.' Another observed, 'Now people have become affluent and can afford more luxuries, that's when they forget about God. Back then no one had work and they were glad to work with the priest. Each Sunday he would call out the names of people to do tasks on particular days. People had nothing else to do.'

I spent an extraordinary day with ordinary people both old and young who knew him. In assessing the man, people were kind, but frank. He was 'never short of a surprise,' observed one. His great weakness was that he did everything himself – he didn't delegate. 'He carried with him a great anger all his life, it was his driving force,' reflected another. Words like impatient, impulsive, and phrases like 'wanted everything done yesterday', and 'not as sensitive as he might have been', to some degree sum up the man. But like all of us, McDyer was a man of his time. Staunchly Republican, he described himself as a 'Christian communist', fiercely opposed to the European Community, yet, as Liam Cunningham remarked, 'If he had been around in the 1990s he would have spent half his time in Brussels!'

Just before he died, one of those who knew him best described his mood as regretful and disillusioned. He felt he had not achieved the co-operation for which he had worked, nor the goodwill of all the people. McDyer knew about the impact of liberation theology elsewhere in the world and admired

> the communal enterprise – people taking into their own hands to build human potential, to build for the future . . . We need "ordinary" people to take power into their own hands and realise the greatness of collective effort. With the zeal of Christ burning within them, they would tear away the accumulated cobwebs of sophistry; they would confound conventional morality with sincerity and they would let the stroke of their challenge ring on the massive shield of the world's hypocrisies and preach the lesson of justice on street corners. This is our greatest immediate need, now.[3]

It was a vision that he himself had not been able to practise, nor that he would live to see.

Like so many, McDyer seemed unable to impart his personal ability to integrate faith and action into a coherent demonstration of Christian living to others. The church in the community remains faithful but fundamentally traditional. The young, and others too, see it as 'theirs' but do not attend it, though many as elsewhere say, 'I have my faith'. But for many, like God, James McDyer is 'very near'.

About ten o'clock that night the present parish priest, Father Eddie Gallagher, called up to see me for some supper at the cottage. He had worked with McDyer, and spoke with affection of the man, and of the need in our day for people of vision. The day with the memory of James McDyer left me with many questions. In the morning eucharist I reflected upon Jonah arriving in Nineveh with news of its imminent destruction, only to find that the people listened to his message and repented, and God forgave them.[4] Jonah was not best pleased, given the hardships he had endured in bringing the message of God to these people. Today I suppose we would say that he did not feel valued. Despite his own misgivings, few could doubt that McDyer's work was valued, and people continue to benefit from his legacy today. Most of us who are in ministry of one kind and another have times of doubt as to whether our ministry is valued, or indeed valuable. What is significant about McDyer, and indeed Jonah, is that both were faithful to their calling. They did what was demanded of them.

For myself there are some lessons to learn and questions to ask. All too often contemporary ministry seems to put too much reliance upon the individual priest. In Glencolumbkille, people spoke warmly of the present parish priest, but also of how tired he was. My brief encounter with him convinced me of that. He was loved because he was there for everyone. Laudable though this might be, I believe such a ministry is unsustainable, and that what is needed in our time is a more total ministry of all of the people. Much lip-service is paid to shared or collaborative ministry, but even here it is possible to observe that its practice is still rather too much like the card dealer who while dealing the cards still holds the pack. Little in ministerial training encourages leadership that empowers others, facilitates community building, or trains folk in how to resolve conflict.

Working for many years in a city where considerable injustice is evident in poor education, low levels of expectation, and all too much unemployment or part-time, low-waged employment, the attraction of a social gospel is considerable. Equally, I found myself asking whether anything in current political ideology really provides for the possibility of creating a world of equity? The demise of socialism, and for all its faults communism, has left an unfilled vacuum. In addition, the theologies of liberation that energised so much in Latin America and elsewhere have failed to ignite theological thought in our Western context, and much of what passes for Christian faith in our time is vapid and frothy.

McDyer managed to unite in himself the twin elements of social action and Christian faith. He did so in a context quite different from our own, and in a sense by holding 'two worlds' together, rather than enabling each to hold the other. Perhaps we need a fresh understanding of the contexts in which our faith is formed in the person of Jesus, as well as in the communities of the early Church. I held this thought in my mind, because in a few weeks' time I would be visiting a more contemporary prophet, my Presbyterian friend Mark Gornik. Here I would see for myself how a venture in urban mission in downtown Baltimore has sought to address this challenge.

There was little doubt in my mind that McDyer had made possible a resurrected community, bringing life out of death. Little doubt too that his own personal witness and energy had led to a community witnessing together a great deal of what it means to work together – 'everyone gives a hand'. Here too was someone like Jesus, impatient with the systems that keep people in oppression and need, and who had responded as Jesus did by saying, 'Stop asking questions, get on with healing.'

McDyer had helped a community to its feet. Without him, the whole history of the south-west of Donegal might have been a very different one. But he, like others before him, including John Wesley, saw that prosperity tends to lead people away from God, rather than towards him. 'I don't see how it is possible,'

Wesley observed, 'in the nature of things, for any true religion to continue long. For religion must necessarily produce industry and frugality, and this cannot but produce riches. But as riches increase so will love of the world, in all its branches.'[5]

Wesley focuses on a very contemporary problem for the Church. Ours is an affluent society in the West, and how we enable gospel events to speak to our present situation in ways that remain true to Jesus' vision of creating a single new humanity under God is important. Almost every movement for renewal begins with some kind of hunger, whether physical or spiritual, or both. Where some kind of bonding takes place, and people do things together, economic and spiritual strength often go hand in hand.

What McDyer practised was essentially an activist faith borne out of a deep conviction of the love of neighbour. World events all too often indicate a planet that is ill at ease with itself, and the past century was probably the deadliest in human history. Within such a world good news has to be proclaimed. On his award of the Nobel Peace Prize, the United Nations Secretary General Kofi Annan observed, 'If today, after the horror of September 11th, we see better and we see further, we will realise that humanity is indivisible.'[6] Perhaps an affluent people need the challenge of self-sacrifice, an economic re-ordering, and a reconciling spirituality.

Whatever is necessary for now, I am glad that I once met the man James McDyer. I have been privileged to learn and share from his heritage, imperfect though it may be. I too believe it is better to 'light ten candles and have nine blow out, than to curse the darkness.'

8

'I arise today . . . through God's strength to pilot me'

Early morning phone calls make me nervous. In my experience they have often brought news that has to some extent been life changing, either because the caller has news of new life, the birth of a baby, or of death. My sojourn in the west of Ireland was rapidly drawing to a close. I had grown to love the wilderness, embracing its changing moods, its light and dark, storm and calm, as my own possession. Each day I woke in the expectation of new insight, new possibilities, even new tasks. On the final Saturday I slept late, and the sun was well up when my wife phoned. She had some news, would I sit down while she read the contents of a letter she had received that morning. It was from 10 Downing Street asking for my permission to allow my name to go to the Queen to become the next Bishop of Bath and Wells.

We talked urgently and somewhat nervously on the phone. Dee was due to join me later to help clear the cottage and begin to make our journey back to London early the following week. We couldn't talk to anyone, and the several hours that it took for her to arrive threw my mind into a maelstrom of questions, practicalities, possibilities and the dawning of the implications for our lives, moving away from London for the first time in over twenty years.

Bath and Wells are twin cities in the County of Somerset in the west of England. The diocese covers much of the ancient boundaries of the county. In the mid 1960s I had founded and led a boys' club for the lads of the Snow Hill estate in Bath. Here too I had become engaged to Dee. We began our early married life in Bristol, in the neighbouring diocese. We had both been teachers there, and I had often taken groups of young people from Ashton Park School into Somerset for orienteering exercises, or to participate in the Duke of Edinburgh Award Scheme. Dee remembered taking her class of five-year-olds to sit on the kerb outside Wells Cathedral to watch the characters on the clock appear at noon and strike the hour. When the twelve strokes had been struck, this solemn little group of children applauded!

'Call on the Lord from a pure heart'

After the phone call I headed for the roof-space chapel, and celebrated the eucharist. The commemoration of the day was for Richard Hooker, Anglican bishop and martyr. I wryly reflected to myself that while 'bishop' was OK, 'martyr' was another thing! Of course to be a 'martyr' in the Christian sense is not necessarily to lay down one's life, save in order to 'bear witness' to truth. As I read the Scriptures that morning, my heart was searching out some 'word' for my own soul. It came in the instructions from St Paul to Timothy, and somehow seemed incredibly appropriate:

> Shun youthful passions and pursue righteousness, faith, love and peace, along with all those who call on the Lord from a pure heart. Have nothing to do with stupid and senseless controversies; you know how they breed quarrels. And the Lord's servant must not be quarrelsome but kindly to everyone, an apt teacher, patient, correcting opponents with gentleness. God may perhaps grant that they will repent and come to know the truth.[1]

I found myself strangely comforted and challenged by those words. If only, I thought, I could model my life as a bishop on them, it would be no mean grace. I began to see that to 'bear witness' to such truth in one's life and ministry is the very foundation of Christian leadership, and I prayed for grace to fulfil such a vocation.

For weeks Slieve League mountain had beckoned us, and it seemed fitting that when Dee arrived we should set off to climb this immense sea cliff as a sort of act of completion of our journey thus far, and a preparation for the journey yet to begin. We did not complete the ascent to the summit. Dee's ankle, which had been weak from an injury incurred on a walk some months previously, began to give us cause for concern at a critical point on a part of the mountain called 'One Man's Pass'. We had two options – to try and return the way we had come, or to head away from the cliff path down into the tooth of the mountain, where there was a pilgrim track leading to a holy site, and where if necessary I could drive the car. After gingerly negotiating rocks, heather, and grassy hummocks, we eventually reached the path as dusk began to fall.

Two choices confronted me, to scramble back up the mountain and down to where we had parked the car, a journey of nearly two miles; or to head for the village and seek to hitch a lift up to Bunglas where the car waited. This was a journey of nearly six miles. I opted to head across the bog and up the mountain, calculating that I would arrive at the car park at sunset. As the clouds darkened the sky early, and I realised that I had no torch, map or compass, I heard my own voice instructing young mountaineers over thirty years ago never to act as foolishly as I was now doing! I was genuinely grateful to God for a safe crossing, and somewhat egotistically proud of my calculations at the accuracy of the journey time! I collected Dee exactly when and where I said I would. That evening we celebrated together looking out across the sea and watching the steady, regular flash of the lighthouse, comforting and warning at the same time of the possibilities and difficulties that lay ahead of us.

Our final morning began with a breaking of bread, an offering of prayers, and then dismantling the 'chapel', cleaning the room, emptying and remaking the fire for an as yet unknown pilgrim to light. I was still surprised at how reluctant I was to leave. The past weeks had been the most amazing oasis of calm and restoration I had ever known in my life, and I knew I was going to need all the grace that had been given to me in this time, together with the joyous rediscovery of the God who is there.

We journeyed to Belfast, having agreed to spend our last day or so with my sister- and brother-in-law and to make a day outing together. We went to Newgrange, a prehistoric passage tomb near Drogheda in the south of Ireland. Newgrange is one of the best preserved of all the Neolithic tombs in the country. It is entered through a low gateway, which has an opening above the lintel to let in the light. Visitors make their way up the passage, which rises about six feet over a distance of a few yards. In the centre of the tomb there is a cross-shaped passage. Here, on the winter solstice, light from the December sun illuminates the passage for nine minutes. It is a remarkable piece of astronomic engineering, and though visitors can ballot to be present at the solstice, electric light provides a simulated presentation for tourists of the effect of the winter sun.

A kind of consecration

After our visit here, we journeyed to the Hill of Slane, the legendary site from which Patrick began his missionary work in Ireland. This has taken on the significance of a holy site for me too. At a similar point of confidentiality in 1997, when I knew I was to be Bishop of Kingston, I had come to Slane with my good friend and spiritual guru, Father Pat Clarke. We had also visited Newgrange that day, and as we climbed the Hill of Slane, I said to Pat, 'I need to tell you, because I want your prayers and blessing – they've decided to make me a bishop.' 'Oh my God,' he replied, 'this needs praying about', and without a moment's hesitation Pat dropped to his knees, and pulled me to mine in the middle of the field before the statue of St Patrick. He prayed for me and blessed me, and placed into my hands a rosary made by a group of displaced Indians in Brazil. 'And do not forget the poor and their humility,' I remember him bidding. It was for me a kind of consecration.

That day too we had climbed to the top of the ruined tower of the ancient Franciscan monastery that once stood here, prayed, and talked about the accident of history that in 1987 had brought us together. I had been visiting Brazil researching the phenomena of basic Christian communities that had emerged among the urban poor. These communities were facilitated by priests and religious in response to the Second Vatican Council's injunction to 'make a preferential gospel option for the poor.' Pat had come to the airport in Sao Paolo to meet me, but messages had got mixed, and I was in fact met by someone else and whisked away. I had seen Pat at the airport, though I did not know it was him then. He had waited all day, and long after the last passenger had left, he had concluded that I had not arrived. Fortunately I was able to call him and we met, as so often with him, in a tiny house in a *favela*, a shanty town on the edge of the city.

At Slane, as we had discussed our common vocation as priests, I reflected on some wisdom from Carl Jung about dealing with preferment:

> It is said that whenever a friend reported enthusiastically, "I have been promoted!" Jung would say, "I'm very sorry to hear that, but if we stick together, I think we will get through it." If a friend arrived depressed and ashamed saying, "I've just been fired," Jung would say, "Let's go open a bottle of wine; this is wonderful news, something good will happen now."[2]

What I think Jung was seeking to address in his hearers was the danger of getting our values wrong. I do not like the use of the term 'preferment' or 'promotion' in relation to Christian ministry. Each office in the Church – whether deacon, priest or bishop – has to be understood as vocation if we are to be faithful to God, who by the consecration of our baptism calls us all to priesthood.

As I contemplated the next step in my vocation, I found Jung's words required of me the responsibility to address the 'dark side' of the self, a self which I for the most part trust. It is right, says Jung, to look at oneself in a 'partially trusting' way, for the human heart is capable of great deceit. I would need people to 'stick together' with me if I were to 'get through' the temptations and vicissitudes of my new calling. And right then I was grateful for Pat's presence, for in the years of our acquaintance he had showed up when I had most needed him to help me see the truth about myself. And as Elisabeth O'Connor once remarked to me, 'Knowing the truth about ourselves makes us humble and open to the truth in the world.'[3]

Around these parts I had discovered was a great place for being 'open to the truth in the world'. A day or so after Pat and I had visited Slane, I had travelled to the Hill of Tara, where a statue commemorates St Patrick's 'legendary visit to the court of King Laoire before he began his mission to bring Christianity to Ireland.' In the window of the now redundant church is the stained glass of Evi Howe's 'Pentecost Window', which symbolises the ever-present possibility of new birth in the Church and in the world. It offers a vision of the restless Spirit of God forever searching for a new humanity, one that would carry out the vision of resurrection.

As I stood at the 'Royal Seat' of the High Kings, the whole of Ireland was spread out like a map. On a beautiful clear day like this one, it was possible to see north-west to Sligo, north-east to the Mountains of Mourne, south to the Dublin mountains and south-west across the plains to Galway and Limerick. Later, the shopkeeper was to tell me that the system of fire beacons ensured that a message could be sent to the whole of Ireland in two seconds. And we are impressed with modern communications! This was the vision that Patrick had, and he dreamed of a people living in harmony under God, a nation witnessing the redemptive love of Christ from coast to coast, from mountaintop to the plains. I too found myself grasping again this longing for my own country and people.

This whole area contains so much that symbolises 'Holy Ireland' that serious pilgrims cannot fail to be touched and moved along a little in their faith. One such site is the town of Kells, famous for the Book of Kells, the magnificently handwritten and illustrated Gospels which now resides in Trinity College Dublin. But here too are High Crosses, majestic structures which contain the story of the gospel within intricately carved stone. When they were first crafted, many crosses contained fine jewels, indicating not only the preciousness with which the Christians regarded these symbols of salvation, but of the value of the gospel itself.

'Be thou my strong tower'

In Kells in 1997 the local priest had organised a pilgrimage around the crosses in his churchyard and the Chapel of Colmkille, which was also in the grounds. Here too was a Round Tower, a symbol of defence in times when communities were threatened by marauding tribes and invaders from the sea. As I made my pilgrimage walk around these crosses, I found myself reflecting on the 'broken' West Cross as signifying something of my own and the world's brokenness. I offered to God my own sinfulness, but also gave thanks for the miracle of salvation which is offered through the One who himself was broken on the cross two thousand years ago. Here too was the East Cross, incomplete, symbol of the incompleteness of all our journeys. The Pilgrim Cross invites pilgrims to face the cross, discovering faith as 'the strong tower' which is a defence, as well as a place for regrouping and rediscovering courage to venture forth in whatever way God leads.

Finally on the walk there was the Cross of Patrick and Columba: a reminder, if one were needed, that others have walked the way of Jesus finding in it both life and hope. Here too is a witness to the resurrection power of God offering a fresh access to the Spirit, symbolised by the Pentecost Window at Tara. Here, amidst so much symbolism of new life and power, I discovered the hope and courage to face my new vocation as a bishop in 1997, and in 2001 I was back at the Hill of Slane. Once again this seemed the place to be. As we mounted the steps of the abandoned tower, and I suffered from my usual bout of vertigo on such ventures, we stood in the cold wind, looked across to the Hill of Tara, the site of the courts of the High King, and sang to the tune of Slane, the Irish traditional hymn, 'Be thou my vision':

> Be thou my vision,
> O Lord of my heart,

Be all else, but naught to me,
Save that thou art.
Be thou my best thought
In the day or the night,
Both waking and sleeping,
Thy presence my light.

The words once again lifted me to my new calling, and as we reached the last verse, they reminded me of the eternal quality of our faith. No High Kings rule Ireland any more, and since St Patrick announced to the pagan king his intention of proclaiming Jesus Christ as the only true 'High King', a thousand monarchs and despots have passed away. Here was evidence, if evidence were needed, that to place confidence in the 'High King of heaven', as the hymn has it, is wisdom not folly. We sang:

High King of heaven,
Thou heaven's bright Sun,
O grant me its joys
After victory is won;
Great heart of my own heart
Whatever befall
Still be thou my vision
Oh! Ruler of all.

From the high point of the Hill of Slane, in the company of loved and special companions, on two occasions there had been the opportunity to meet with God and to review my calling. This was my mount of Transfiguration, and while no dazzling white, or dramatic 'voice from heaven' was heard, it has become a place of quiet affirmation. Like many people I have encountered God on the mountains. From Moses to Jesus, the Bible records any number of occasions where people sought to interpret their calling in the light of such meetings, and Christian history is littered with such moments in the lives of saints, official and unofficial.

'This is my Son, the Chosen One. Listen to him'

As Jesus prepared to journey into Jerusalem and face the consequences of his choice to do God's will made in the desert some years before, he too ascended a mountain. Jesus' mission faced increasing opposition from the authorities. Herod, his cousin John the Baptist's old enemy, was making threatening noises. At the same time, Jesus himself was fulfilling the promise of bringing good news to the poor, feeding the hungry, healing the sick and symbolically driving out the forces of oppression in places as divergent as Roman-occupied Gerasa, as well as facing the intransigence of religious leaders.[4] The decision taken in the desert to 'do homage to the Lord your God' and to serve him alone,[5] had taken its toll, and Jesus needed encouragement.

On the mountain top Jesus was accompanied by Peter, James and John. They became witnesses to a remarkable summit conference between God's top people – Moses, Elijah and Jesus. 'A voice came from the cloud',[6] and the disciples, even the garrulous Peter, were reduced to silence. Something significant was happening. When Elijah was in trouble he too went to the mountains for refuge.[7] Instead he was given strength by God to return to the struggle against the forces that threatened to eliminate the worship of the true and living God. On another mountain, Sinai, God gave Moses the commandments for creating a just nation. When in due course the people refused to practise them, Moses, devastated by the rejection, returned to the mountain for solace and consolation.[8]

Jesus and his disciples are depicted as being in the company of people who have been in the struggle, who have been faithful to God, and have sought to fulfil their vocation as signs of hope and bearers of good news. They too faced the pain of opposition, sometimes from the very people who had most reason to benefit from their faithfulness to God, but more often from the representatives of 'the principalities and ruling forces who are masters of darkness in this world'.[9]

God's encouragement and re-affirmation of Jesus as 'Chosen One' was as much a message for the witnesses of this theophany as Jesus himself. The watching disciples saw how the 'aspect of

[Jesus'] face . . . changed and his clothing became sparkling white.'[10] The dazzling whiteness of the clothing symbolised martyrdom, and Jesus knew this was his destiny. But whiteness symbolises resurrection too, and Jesus promises his hearers they will witness his rising again[11] if they remain faithful. The disciples wanted a permanent memorial of the summit meeting: they decided to build three shelters, so that in the future they and other pilgrims could come and stand on the site and marvel at the event.

It would be easy to criticise the disciples. Poor old things, we might think, they have misunderstood as usual – this is not a time for doing but for listening. The same voice that spoke on Sinai, and in the stillness to Elijah, now repeated the words spoken at Jesus' baptism, 'This is my Son, my Chosen One. Listen to him.' As someone who is inclined to activism, I rather think that I would have joined the disciples in wanting to *do* something. But the act of listening is an essential prerequisite for any action. Jesus' own act of 'listening' was at its most focused in the wilderness, where he not only heard the voice of the tempter, but re-engaged with the living Word of God, as he sought to understand his vocation.

The previous weeks had been an opportunity to listen to God's 'Chosen One'. I could not have anticipated the events of the past few days, and the 'listening' that was done was against the wider backdrop of my vocation in general. But as I too was on the mountain once again, I found that I needed the encouragement of God's voice amidst the clamour of other voices, other claims. As someone whose personality demands the 'filling of the shining hour', I am an easy prey to other voices. I am easily busied, and sometimes that busyness, rather than leading to clarity, leads to confusion. Even during precious days of solitude, I had been all too easily stirred up and thrown around.

Clarence Jordan, author of the *Cotton Patch Gospels,* an interpretation of the New Testament from the perspective of the poor in the southern states of America, reflects at one point on the Greek word for devil – *diabolos.* The word 'comes from *dia* meaning "around through" and *bollo* meaning "to throw" from the English word "ball". *Diabolos* means "one who throws things about" – one who stirs things up – gets them confused. The work of the devil is to get us muddled.'[12] Since that fateful day in September 2001 the world of the comfortable, secure West has been thrown about, stirred up and confused. For many millions within our world, they are thrown about like this every day.

Like Jesus' first disciples, we are invited to 'take up the cross', to bear something of the weight of human sin and suffering along with Jesus. Simply, we cannot reach the hope of the resurrection, the defeat of all that is destructive and hateful, without cost. The twin images at the transfiguration, of the whiteness of the robes as symbols of both martyrdom and resurrection, remind me that, for all the excitement and anticipation of a new ministry, there will be a cost experienced in misunderstanding and resistance, as well as when the occasional prophetic word has to be spoken. There is a cost too in the bearing of the disappointment of others, as well as the encouragement of those who are disheartened or disillusioned.

When Jesus descended from the mountain, having experienced the assurance of God's continued blessing upon his ministry, he was immediately thrust into the chaos and confusion of the world. Here he faced the convulsing deaf mute boy, whose 'possession by the devil' symbolised the presence of disbelief not only in the world, but also among the disciples who are 'thrown about' by Jesus' insistence that the journey to resurrection is by way of the cross.

'I arise today . . . through the strength of Heaven'

Some of this went through my mind that early winter afternoon as we passed the statue of St Patrick on our return to the car, and the journey to Belfast. Some years before I had been sitting in a chapel in the Marino Institute in Dublin for a short service of prayer and music. Here for the first time I heard the beautiful voice of Rita Connolly singing from Kuno Meyo's translation of 'The Deer's Cry', an eighth-century poem ascribed to St Patrick, and sometimes called 'St Patrick's Breastplate'. It is a prayer-poem which has served as a prayer of protection for pilgrims and other travellers, but I have found in it something that connects me to the God who chooses, calls and strengthens against the 'one who throws things about':

I arise today

Through the strength of Heaven
Light of sun
Radiance of moon
Splendour of fire
Speed of lightning
Swiftness of wind
Depth of the sea
Stability of earth
Firmness of rock

I arise today
Through God's strength to pilot me
God's eye to look before me
God's wisdom to guide me
God's way to lie before me
God's shield to protect me
From all who wish me ill
Afar and anear
Alone and in a multitude
Against every cruel merciless power
That may oppose my body and soul

Christ with me, Christ before me,
Christ behind me, Christ in me,

Christ beneath me, Christ above me,
Christ on my right, Christ on my left,
Christ when I lie down, Christ when I sit down,
Christ when I arise, Christ to shield me

Christ in the heart of everyone who thinks of me

Christ in the mouth of everyone who speaks of me
I arise today.[13]

My 'descent' from the mountain was indeed into a form of chaos. The following week was a blur of meetings, medical inspections, visits to the new diocese, press conferences and family reunions. Dee and I had initially intended to keep this window of time very short, so that I could wash my clothes, repack my bags and head off to New York within forty-eight hours or so of returning home. It was not to be the period of domestic order that we had planned. The trip to New York had to be postponed for several days, and when eventually I slumped into my seat on the Virgin Airbus 340 it was as a wiser, but more tired man!

9

'Journeying outwards – and inwards'

My first flight was in a Dakota DC3 Cambrian Airways plane from Bristol to Belfast in the summer of 1964. It was at one and the same time the most wonderful and painful experience. In the days before pressurisation of aircraft cabins was common place, the aircraft covered the four hundred or so miles at little over 8000 feet. Despite all the advice to pinch my nose, yawn and suck sweets I suffered painful earache for much of the flight. However, the wonder of it for me was gazing out of the window as the country and then the Irish Sea unfolded beneath us. I was hooked. From then on, whenever asked at airport check-in 'which seat – window or aisle?' the answer has been unfailingly 'window'.

Since then I have travelled the world mostly near the back of the plane in the cheap seats. Economy seating has become the equivalent of steerage on the emigrant ships. Whenever my travel plans allow, I choose to fly during the day. Although modern flying has had most of its romance removed, what with the endless procession of movie and audio channels, carefully timed drinks and food service, so that one is rarely left with one's own thoughts for long, nevertheless with a window seat one can from time to time glimpse the passing world.

My first transatlantic flight many years ago held something of that sense of adventure, for me at least, that has inspired all travellers. The captain pointed out the way marks, the Blasket Islands off the west of Ireland, and about halfway across the ocean drew our attention to the *QE2* sailing majestically below us. Cloud covered northern Canada, but he was soon making us aware of the Maine coast, Boston, and then passing around towards Kennedy Airport we glimpsed the Manhattan skyline.

Now I was travelling the route for the umpteenth time. 'No window seats, I'm afraid,' said the clerk at the check-in desk, 'only one in the centre.' The perils of changing one's flight, I thought – and to a night journey too! Despite advice given me when I was General Secretary of USPG always to fly economy 'to keep your feet on the ground', I tried to get an upgrade. 'Sir,' said the clerk, 'you can't buy an upgrade with the ticket you're flying on.' She gave me a look that indicated I was lucky, given the price I had paid for it, not to be strapped to the wing for the duration!

However, even in today's packaged flying there are moments of sheer wonderment available to the discerning traveller, even in the spit and sawdust section of the plane. After being told to pull our blinds down on one bright sunny morning flight to New York so that people could see the movie, I dozed for a couple of hours until it was finished. Awaking, I found the screen had grown dark, and I cautiously lifted the shutter to gaze out upon a majestic scene of blue, green, black and the occasional brown and white of tiny houses. We were flying down the coast of Newfoundland, with its tiny shore-hugging communities. From 35,000 feet the most beautiful backdrop of hinterland comprising inlets, lakes, mountains and a seemingly endless blue iciness evoked memories of heroic stories of explorers of long ago. I remember recalling how journeys over territory that took past generations lives and lifetimes to cross now took only a few fleeting seconds, with all sense of wonder and mystery lost in the trash of yet another long-haul flight.

Two landscapes

During my sojourn in Donegal I had occasionally turned to Barry Lopez, whose writings, as I have mentioned, in one form or another always accompany my pilgrimage. He had spent long days in landscapes like those being crossed on my flight, albeit now in the darkness. Whereas in the past I had gazed on this landscape from the heavens, he had observed it with the meticulousness of someone squinting into a microscope.

He writes not only of mixes of colour, smells and events leading to lost wonderment, but to dreams of 'respectful human participation in a landscape, generation after generation. Dreams of need and fulfillment. Common enough dreams. Poignant, ineffable, indefensible, the winds of an interior landscape.'[1] And this particular dream is expressed in 'a handful of beautiful damp stones in arctic sunlight, a green duck feather stuck to one finger. Water dripping back to the river. I fumble at some prayer here I have forgotten, utterly forgotten, how to perform. I place the stones back in the river as carefully as possible, and move inland to sleep.'

Despite my jumbled weariness and excitement brought about through the unexpected events of the previous few days appearing like a tornado out of an apparently cloudless sky, I was beginning to think my way back into my retreat, which was now to be more of a movement from solitude into community. The following days would expose me more to people, events and places than the past several weeks had done. I questioned how I would cope. Would I make the synthesis between the exterior and the interior aspects of my life? I had become used to rhythms, patterns of prayer and an interiority of life that now had to be interpreted against the more raw-edged, 'in your face' nature of New York and its relentless energy.

Lopez helped me here: 'I think of two landscapes,' he observes, 'one outside the self, the other within. The external landscape is the one we see – not only the line and colour of the land and its shading at different times of the day, but also its plants and animals in season, its weather, its geology, the record of its climate and evolution.' To some extent this has been part of my experience over the past few weeks. I anticipate a change in landscape: not only to one of skyscrapers and mean streets, and the endless variety of Homo sapiens, but of parks, museums, city riverside walks, as well as changed landscapes, empty spaces and 'Ground Zero'.

'The second landscape I think of,' says Lopez, 'is an interior one, a kind of projection within a person of a part of the exterior landscape.' He speaks of relationships being influenced by 'winter light falling on a particular kind of granite, or the effect of humidity on the frequency of the blackpoll warbler's burst of song.' For one who was used to the busyness of urban life, and for whom the occasional glimpse of light on a wall or tree, or the habits of a garden or wild bird held little more than a passing interest, seeing such connectedness was something I was all too unaware of, yet I was learning to appropriate within my self. 'That these relationships have purpose and order, however inscrutable they may seem to us, is a tenet of evolution,' observes Lopez. 'Similarly the speculations, intuitions, and formal ideas we refer to as "mind" are a set of relationships in the interior landscape with purpose and order; some of them are obvious, many impenetrably subtle.'

I sensed that Lopez was somehow speaking to me about the apparent incongruity of the various elements of my life at that time, but also about the incongruity of a humanity violated. How much of modern 'manwomanhood's'[2] alienation and despair was the result of the disruption of either the exterior or interior landscape? Not only were there 'obvious' and 'subtle' elements to our 'interior landscape', caused by 'speculations' and 'intuitions', but also what Lopez refers to as 'the shape and character of these relationships in a person's thinking.' These

> are deeply influenced by where on this earth one goes, what one touches, the patterns one observes in nature – the intricate history of one's life in the land, even a life in the city, where wind, the chirrup of birds, the line of the falling leaf, are known. These thoughts are arranged further according to the thread of one's moral, intellectual, and spiritual development. The interior landscape responds to the character and subtlety of an exterior landscape; the shape of the individual mind is affected as much by land as it is by genes.[3]

Low grade depression

Having lived on the edge of the world for a few weeks in a place where every local knew and understood the signs that marked the changes in the weather, the climate and their impact upon the environment, I prepared myself to enter an atmosphere where the price of everything was known, but the subtleties and vagaries of nature were barely glimpsed, save for extreme heat or cold. I sensed the coming weeks would face me with some difficulties in holding together the interior and exterior aspects of my life. The Donegal days had released the possibility of an intimacy of relationship with God, my environment and the people whose paths I had all too fleetingly crossed. Would such intimacy be possible here – and indeed should it be?

Immigration controls at JFK were surprisingly relaxed. The last flight of the evening, perhaps. The welcome was warm, even friendly: 'Thank you for visiting with us at this time,' remarked the normally cool immigration officer. 'You're welcome,' I found myself saying, slipping all too easily into that transatlantic-ese that so often passes for courtesy, but is all too often flip discourtesy.

'There is a sort of low grade depression here,' remarked the taxi driver as he took my travelling companion and me into Manhattan. We passed within a few blocks of Ground Zero. The streets were strangely quiet, and as the door opened to set down my fellow passenger, I picked up the strong smell one associates with chemical pollution. 'That's what it's been like here since 9–11,' commented the driver. A few days later I was to discover at closer quarters the leaden poisonous stench amidst the still smouldering ruins of the World Trade Center.

New York is not a city I have associated with depression during the many visits I have made here. Normally it has a buzz, a kind of twenty-four-hour excitement, a place where anything and everything is available – 'twenty-four seven three six five', as I have heard its round-the-clock, round-the-year lifestyle described. Of course much remained like this, shopping at the corner store, or buying a pizza at two in the morning was still very much within the lifestyle of New Yorkers. Yet beneath the apparent normality there lay a sense of something more than lives and buildings lost, and coupled with it a questioning: of values, of the nature and place of politics, even of the meaning of life itself.

I arrived at my friends Rita and Mark Gornik just before midnight. Knowing they had a somewhat wakeful one-year-old, I tapped the door with quiet insistence until they heard. Despite the lateness of the hour, and what I was to discover as frequently interrupted nights, we caught up with each other's news and the impact of events upon us. They spoke with real pain about the events of '9–11', of the fear that swept the city, of the loss of innocence, of the feelings of vulnerability, of the unease about the retaliation, and yet expressed an impotence as to the viability of any other alternatives. Like the taxi driver, they too spoke about 'depression'.

Mark and I had first met in El Salvador during the dirty war of the 1980s, when death squads roamed the streets and regularly left the mangled and shot remains of human beings piled like so much garbage to maintain a reign of terror in cities, towns and villages across the land. These actions, it was said, had the implicit approval and support of counter-insurgency bodies within the United States government. A slogan scrawled in Spanish on the walls of the US Embassy in San Salvador read 'Here they plan the deaths of our people'.

It had been a traumatic time, forcing us to ask many questions about how people who have been oppressed for many years obtain their freedom. We had questioned the role of superpowers in supporting oppressive regimes out of fear of 'communism' or 'capitalism'. The Berlin Wall and the status of the Soviet Union had remained largely unchallenged. We had spoken briefly over dinner that first night in San Salvador in 1988, but being among the last down to breakfast I had not, unlike Mark, ventured outside our hotel that morning. His first words to me were, 'Man, I've been arrested.' He had bidden me look out of the window to see the ranks of security police who had surrounded our hotel.

Mark's arrest had lasted little more than a few minutes, but it should have been expected. We had been advised to enter the country as 'tourists'. At the time this was an unlikely designation, and I, who was carrying BBC sound recording equipment for reports I was presenting on the World Service's *World Religion* programme, made my designation as a tourist highly suspect. Later in the day some Americans staying in the same hotel had been interrogated for some hours by the Treasury Police. On our return from some visits to churches and charity groups our fellow residents had been anxious to tell us of their experience and of what we had missed.

Mark is quite unlike anyone else I have ever met. In 1988, at twenty-eight years old he was already two years into New Song, one of the most ambitious church and community programmes I have ever witnessed. A native of Baltimore, Mark had grown up as a middle-class kid in the suburbs. He was attached to the Presbyterian Church of America, a small, relatively conservative denomination, whose seminaries tended to train expository preachers rather than community activists. By the time we met, Mark's vocation in ministry had led him to Sandtown, a poor, largely African-American district of Baltimore. In 1986 the highest rates of infant mortality in the city, lead poisoning, school failure, and eviction were the reality of this neighbourhood. Each year some 300 people were murdered, usually as a result of shootings, health care was virtually non existent, and many of the streets marked by boarded-up properties, which became breeding grounds for drug dealers and takers, as well as a ready source of fuel for arsonists. For many, the neighbourhood represented its own 'Ground Zero' – a place of devastation, loss, death and hopelessness. Like Ground Zero, Sandtown was a place we were planning to visit in the coming days.

That night, however, was for sleeping; new journeys could be planned the next day.

Adjusting the pace

I discovered early that my room for the next few weeks was a thoroughfare. A lounge extension, it was Mark and Rita's baby Peter's playroom. No chance of a chapel here – and given his pattern of waking and sleeping, little chance of solitude either. At first I found this strange, even a little annoying. I, who had been used to my own company, making my own life and determining the extent of my devotions within the privileged intimacy of seclusion, was now faced by immediacy, the demands and needs of others. Over the following weeks I was to discover the daily reality for many good, believing people, who seek to live their lives of faith against the backdrop of unrelenting pressures of work, the demands of family and modern living. I would ask, with them, how do we experience God in all this?

Rita, a Hungarian doctor specialising in addiction, had a busy and demanding job in a hospital in the Bronx. Mark was working to found a seminary which will specifically train people to work in multicultural environments, developing a practical 'city theology', offering biblical reflection and social action borne out of understanding of the context both of community and the Scripture. Baby Peter was lovingly parented, and bilingually educated by parents and a delightful Hungarian childminder who was more like a doting grandmother.

The two-minute walk to the local deli for a coffee and bagel reminded me why I love this place so much. Within seconds one is into the multicultural reality of little communities. This one bordered on Harlem, long known for its African-American residents. However, for the coming weeks I would be served here by an American of Korean origin, and later my wife would arrive in a taxi driven by a Vietnamese. Despite its reputation for surliness, I have found far more conversation, sense of community on the sidewalks of New York than my own native London. Largely, the absence of big supermarket chains and the impossibility of driving anywhere here means that people shop locally, and they walk.

Suddenly I was faced with time to fill. In the previous few weeks this had not been difficult. I now realised that this time in my sabbatical was a sort of 'redeeming moment' – a time for enjoyment, for giving and receiving from others, and perhaps for relaxing from over-zealousness. Being me, it would have its busyness, but not necessarily in an over-focused way. On my way to Central Park, I passed a housing project. It is built in the name of one of the great Black American philanthropists, and outside are printed the words 'There is no growth without struggle'. I sensed this imperative was urged upon African Americans as they sought for equality of opportunity and rights, but I saw it for myself as an injunction for my journeyings there. Now I was no longer protected by isolation, my own carefully planned hermitage, and the need only to care for myself. Here I would need to adapt, fit in, attempt an unprotected spirituality, discern a different kind of holiness, find hope against much that was hopeless.

'The art that is life'

As the sun shone with unexpected warmth I walked and sat in Central Park before making my way, as I do almost by habit, to the American wing of the Metropolitan Museum of Art. Here I spent a half hour or so contemplating the transposed living-room of one of architect Frank Lloyd Wright's houses. I understand little about architecture despite once, briefly, considering it as a career. What fascinates me about Lloyd Wright's work is the way in which he seeks to design the building to 'become an integral part of the landscape, rather than an un-related element.' This integration he called 'organic architecture'. I sensed that I was drawn to this because I was trying to bring together the different dimensions of my life, as well as to try and understand something of the cosmic need for integrity between us humans and this landscape of which we are related elements.

My first encounter with Frank Lloyd Wright's work came around the time when I was struggling to put bits and pieces of my disjointed life together. It had been during my visit to New York back in the mid 1980s, when I was using the United States as a springboard to journeying to Latin and South America to explore the growing phenomena of liberation theology and its expression in the Church of the poor – the base ecclesial communities. I had begun that particular journey thinking that it was primarily exterior, looking away from the interior, the inner self. But I had soon discovered that no outward journey can be made without an inner journey too.

I remember this coming as a particular shock. Certainly I had planned to take companions on the journey, as I do now, and among them was Gerard Hughes and his book *In Search of A Way*, and William Least-Heat Moon's *Blue Highways*. After the initial excitement of 'Biting into the Big Apple' back then, I found myself strangely disconcerted. I had been grabbing at all the experience, insight and perception in everything I had seen, people I met and things that I had heard. Then, inexplicably at the time, I found myself lonely, not a little afraid. I had left behind unresolved issues in the parish, and I was dealing with other personal struggles. Some words from Gerry Hughes had leapt off the page as if they were meant for me, though he was recalling what some of his friends had once said to him –'I don't think you know who you are.'[4] I realised that this was true for me at that time – that my life had little sense of integration. The exterior and interior elements of it were disconnected.

I had looked then at the journey ahead. I was about to enter the violent neighbourhoods of a number of US cities, as well as the war-torn environments of Central America, and eventually, for the first time, the poverty and desperation of the *favelas*. Had I the resources emotionally and spiritually to cope with it? Who am I kidding? I wondered to myself. Then I had discovered something that I have almost taken for granted now, namely that it is often the unexpected encounter or experience that provides the fusion needed in bringing the whole person together.

Lloyd Wright was not formally part of what became known as the Arts and Crafts movement, but the philosophy behind his work of integrating architecture and landscape was similar in intent. This movement sprang from the work of a group of reformers who were passionately committed to righting the ills of an increasingly industrialised and urban society. They chose the arts as their medium from which to make their challenge. Convinced that industrialists had caused the degradation of work and the destruction of the environment by reducing formerly creative craftsmen and women to anonymous labourers mindlessly repeating the same unfulfilling tasks, they sought a revival of craftsmanship. Along with this revival, they sought more satisfying working conditions and 'the promotion of simple uncluttered interiors achieved through unification of all art forms.'[5] In 1987 I had made my first visit to the Boston Museum of Fine Arts and *The Art that is Life* exhibition, celebrating 'The Arts and Crafts Movement in America'. Here I had found the external impetus to my thinking and reflecting, enabling me to begin to see then that the exterior and interior elements of life need a cohesion, a synthesis, if we are truly to live hopefully.

From receiving to giving

I reflected on all this as I made my way back to my new home on West End Avenue, crossing the Park in the still warm evening sunshine. Here families and other groups of people were playing games, walking dogs, or sitting like me enjoying an evening in the sun a mere few blocks from the devastation of Ground Zero. Was this, I wondered, 'living hopefully'? Or was it just that in the face of such mind-blowing horrors, denial is the only way our psyche has of dealing with such things? And if this is true of things that happen on our own doorstep, so to speak, how much easier is it to close off other inhumanities that ravage our world?

I was musing a little over this while waiting later in the evening for an old school friend of one of my sons to join me for dinner. This man in his thirties I had known in his teens as a good rugby player and a fine athlete. Now working in New York, he had witnessed at first hand the events of September 11. He spoke of how these had affected him. 'I am not a person of faith,' he observed, 'although I have been attracted by the kind of faith about which you talk,' he kindly continued. 'What September 11 did for me was to make me sure about two things: first, that there should be no revenge and, second, I needed to do something useful with my life. If I had a faith, I wouldn't want it to be based on need – I am not needy; I am successful and I love life. Any faith that I would want to embrace would be one that demanded me to do something for others.' Of course I have collated elements of the conversation, but I was incredibly moved by this man, touched by his honesty, excited at the prospect of someone who, after receiving much and literally looking disaster in the face, wanted to re-orientate his life from receiving to giving.

Our conversation ranged over many things, and I felt myself to be extraordinarily privileged to be in his company. He asked for some suggestions of things to read, particularly in the light of some elements of our conversation about undeserved suffering, how it is possible to believe in God, and most surprisingly of all, praying. For me this encounter was a gift, a sort of sign, an indication that on my pilgrimage a synthesis between the exterior and the interior was possible, affirming once again that God was all, and in all.

10

A New Song

Railways have a habit of passing some of the most deprived neighbourhoods as they enter North American cities. Mark and I had caught the early morning Metroliner from Grand Central Station to Baltimore, Maryland. Some people come alive when they enter the countryside, observing with almost childlike joy the sight of green fields, rivers, hills and the like. Mark is the only person I know who becomes animated at the sight of redundant warehouses, boarded-up and graffiti-decorated housing projects, whether of terraces or tower blocks. As we passed first into Philadelphia and then into Baltimore, Mark kept up a running commentary on the possibilities, the ventures that had been tried, or where he knew nothing about the local situation, the possibilities, a vision of what might be. I was inspired and happy for him – it was as if, like a fish in a tank, he had suddenly been released into the stream and was swimming with new vigour, new hope.

Fresh out of seminary in 1986 Mark, together with his friends Alan and Susan Tibbells, moved into the neighbourhood of Sandtown, in Mark's native Baltimore. But this was a kid from the suburbs, and he was on new, unfamiliar turf. Alan, his co-worker and fellow visionary, is a quadriplegic, having broken his back playing in a basketball game. It was through Alan that Mark came to faith, together they discovered their vocation to the urban poor. The decision to go to Sandtown was the result of long discussions on the question: 'What would it mean for us to follow Christ in Baltimore city, a city racially divided and increasingly home to the region's abandoned poor?' In their deliberations, both men had been helped by the African American theologian pastor, John Perkins, the founder of the Christian Community Development Association.

The 3 Rs of Relocation, Reconciliation, *and* Redistribution

Perkins had grown up in the inner city. Here too he had ministered and come to believe that if the gospel of Jesus Christ is to be taken seriously, then the question, 'How did Jesus love?'[1] has to be both asked and answered. Perkins himself was convinced that the answer lay in learning the '3Rs' of *Relocation, Reconciliation* and *Redistribution.* Jesus' first act of loving was one of relocation, expressed in his coming to earth to live as part of humanity. Gornik recognised that if he were 'to follow the way of Christ' it would be essential to live in the community where there is self-evident need for change. Living presence is the source of the church's strength. In his book *To live in Peace* Mark reflected in a footnote: '*Relocation* can sometimes be used by Christians to assume a sense of moral and intellectual superiority over the people of the community. Instead of being neighbours, it can be another exploitative "missionary" pose. Relocation is more complex than we imagine and more fraught with danger to Christ's name than has been acknowledged.'[2]

The Tibbells and Gornik relocated by renting houses in the area. In Baltimore there are some 40,000 vacant houses. For several months they simply hung around the streets of the neighbourhood becoming known and getting to know their neighbours and the community. A family of white people and a single white guy moving into a virtual black ghetto caused considerable curiosity. Mark observed, 'Some folks thought we were drug dealers, others that we were cops, and we weren't sure which group might shoot us first!'

To the question, 'What are you doing here?' their reply was always, 'We are here to be neighbours.' Gradually trust was won, and a small group met in Gornik's house. Theologically, the two men described their strategy as seeking to place their lives at the service of the community. Rather than develop their own programmes, they sought to make the wisdom of St Paul their practice for mission:

> [We] did not come with any brilliance of oratory or wise argument to announce to you the mystery of God. [We] resolved that the only knowledge (we) would have while [we] were with you was knowledge of Jesus, and of him as crucified Christ. [We] came among you in weakness, in fear and great trembling and what [we] spoke was not meant to convince by philosophical argument, but to demonstrate the convincing power of the Spirit, so that your faith should depend not on human weakness, but on the power of God.[3]

Their choice of suspending all 'knowledge', 'oratory' and 'wise argument', together with their decision to see the cross of self-giving as the means by which new life might become possible, enabled them to respond to people's request first for a church. Neighbours were invited to 'come as you are' into Gornik's home. Here prayers were made for the needs in the families and among the neighbours. As the Bible was read, everyone was invited to share in reflection on passages, particularly from Luke, Nehemiah and Isaiah, that seemed to speak most to their present situation. The Scriptures chosen included those about 'restoring the streets' and of 'healing', 'binding up the broken-hearted'. 'Everything revolved around building community together,' said Mark of this time.

The breakthrough came one Sunday evening as folk gathered to reflect on the pain of the neighbourhood. 'That night,' observed Gornik, 'our small congregation set out to be urban planners and visionaries. We took out coloured pencils and sheets of paper, and began to ask ourselves, "What is God's dream for our community?" ' For several hours ideas flowed, papers got filled, a number of possibilities formed themselves into a series of questions:

> Why not a community that provides jobs and develops businesses?
>
> Why not a landscape filled with newly planted trees and no more vacant houses?

Why not a focus on middle-school-aged youth that would grow into job training and scholarships?

Why not medical help for those with addiction problems?

The list went on, and so did the dreaming. In the pictures houses were empty no longer; the streets were named almost biblically 'Hope' and 'No Drugs'. 'Yet,' said Mark, 'looking around the room there was not one skilled construction worker, nor medical professional, nor anyone with financial means.'

Within a short while goals began to be set. The first of these was highly ambitious: to eliminate vacant housing in the community by creating affordable homes for everyone in Sandtown. This goal was to be achieved in part through working with Habitat for Humanity, a charity founded by Millard Fuller. Here potential 'owners', in exchange for 'sweat equity' and the help of volunteers as well as professionals, are provided with a home purchased over twenty years with mortgage repayments no greater than the lowest rents available in the community. 'Sweat equity' is the means by which a person uses their labour in exchange for a cash down-payment, and typically amounts to 500 hours per house.

When I first visited Sandtown in 1989, the elements of this vision for 're-habbing' houses were being put in place. There had been great rejoicing a few weeks previously when the first Habitat house was occupied by its 'sweat equity' owner. Her name was Sonia Street, and she continues to work on Habitat projects around her community and in the wider world. In the street of terraced houses, many with boarded windows and blackened doors, the re-habbed house looked like a shining new crown in a row of rotten teeth.

Revisiting Sandtown in November 2001, I was moved to see the whole street now rebuilt, along with several others, parking lots for cars outside, and a real pride in the neighbourhood. To date some 280 houses have been refurbished, and the goal by 2003 is to complete five hundred such homes. 'By 2001,' observed Gornik, 'Habitat was building at a rate of fifty houses per year. In this they have gained not only the moral, but the practical and economic support of former president, Jimmy

Carter, who was regularly to be seen on a work detail in Sandtown neighbourhood.'

Reconciliation

This did not happen instantly, neither did it happen in isolation. The commitment by the founders of New Song to Perkins' '3Rs' called for a new way of being church. Growing 'church' in this context required a deep understanding of the sense of abandonment of the people both economically and racially. People gradually began to see that the relocation that had been a key element of Gornik and Tibbells' calling had to be more than a gesture. It had to become part of the rehabilitation programme within the neighbourhood. But mere rebuilding and the provision of affordable housing would not tackle by itself the underlying bitterness, sense of betrayal and neglect experienced by Sandtown's residents. This was, and remains a spiritual, economic and social problem.

In Sandtown the task of *reconciliation*, 'that which is at the heart of the Christian story,' said Gornik, 'had to become integral to our effective witness in the community. Enfolded in the story of a sinful people being forgiven and reconciled to a holy God, the church has to embrace, love, forgive and incorporate people across all barriers of gender, ethnicity, race, culture and class.' The vision for New Song was to build a community of children, teenagers and adults in the neighbourhood from among those who believed themselves disenfranchised by both Church and society.

New Song set out to make church such that it could be at the centre of community regeneration. It was to be the worshipping community of faith that would encourage belief in the possibility of change. Here too people would find the support they would need to keep going, overcome differences, and come to believe that the risks, which were not inconsiderable, were worth taking. Reconciliation became a way of life, rather than a programme. The difference was to be made in the ordinary, daily commitment to refuse to put up with things as they were.

Three stories in particular illustrated this for me. During my

November 2001 visit I was introduced to a young black man, Anton, who now works for the Eden project, a New Song ministry that provides employment advice and opportunities within the community, who told me that he had grown up in the neighbourhood. Growing up in its mean streets, like many others he had 'done drugs', arson, and been into a whole bunch of other criminal activity for which he eventually received a prison sentence. Returning to the community after doing his time, he said that he felt he was living 'somewhere else'. His neighbourhood had re-habbed houses where once he had done drugs; here too was a pre-school, and after-school club for so-called school failures, and there was even the beginnings of health care in the community. He decided that he wanted to be part of whatever was going on. He became part of the church, and seems to have experienced a deep conversion both to God and the neighbourhood, and has become a key activist in the renewal of Sandtown.

As he spoke to me, I reflected on the passage from John's Gospel on the story of the man born blind[4] that I had been considering some weeks before during my isolation and retreat in Ireland. Here was part of 'humanity born blind', as the original Greek puts it, giving testimony to his community in much the same way as the man Jesus encountered had done: 'I was blind but now I can see.' When Mark Gornik describes the *charis*[5] or the 'gift' of New Song, he speaks of it as 'a neighbourhood way of being church that seeks to bring God's liberating reign to all dimensions of life, calling people to work together for the peace of the neighbourhood and the city.' Anton was a living example of that gift.

The second story concerned the first couple to be married in the New Song church, Orlando and Teresa Mobuary. Like all parents, they wanted their children to grow up in a safe and thriving community. Following their marriage, Orlando began working part time for Habitat; eventually he learnt a trade as an electrician, and became the construction manager. Orlando carried the responsibility for the quality of the houses, and in no small measure the overall effectiveness of the ambitious programme would depend upon his attention to detail.

When I visited in 1988, and again in 1991, a project was being worked on that would eventually create what was to become known as the New Song Learning Center. This purpose-built school and neighbourhood facility was managed by Susan Tibbells and had excellent resources and facilities. Orlando and Teresa's children attended school and took part in its varied activities. A few blocks up the street was the Health Center, where the family had their medical needs attended to. For Gornik:

> This is the sort of transforming difference that is being made for families on every block in the Sandtown focus area.
>
> When I think of the process thus far, there are many stories that bring hope and encouragement, among the most important to me is the story of Isaac Newman – Ike to his friends. This young man first said out loud that we should start a church, and was the first individual to work on our building. He is not only integrally involved in the overall life of New Song, but is also a Habitat employee. For fifteen years he has been rebuilding his community and helping his family and neighbourhood. In December 2000, Ike became a Habitat homeowner. That is what New Song is all about.[6]

I was delighted to renew my acquaintance with Ike, whom I met first as a teenager and as Mark's neighbour.

Reborn neighbourhood – sign of resurrection

These stories illustrate that the *charis* of New Song was accomplished through a spirit of celebration, common life, and community development worked out at the neighbourhood level. Whenever a new resident took the keys for their new home, there was an act of dedication and celebration on the streets. This became a vital part of the church's witness to the community. Not unlike the early Church recorded in the Acts of the Apostles they praised God, 'having favour with all the people. And the Lord added to their number day by day those who were being saved.'[7]

Part of my sabbatical pilgrimage was to discern signs of hope in the midst of the catastrophe of much of modern living. As I wandered these streets with Mark, Ike, Alan, Susan, Laverne, Anton and others, I saw the living reality of resurrection life, not only in renewed individuals, empowered no doubt by the grace of God, but of a re-born neighbourhood. Could it be that somewhat less than fifteen years before no adequate health care provision had been made for the people of this community, and yet now there was a health centre that provided affordable medical provision for six thousand? And what of the young people, mainly black, who had been marked 'school failure', yet who now had both the resources and the inspiration to think in terms of college, of career, of future?

Here I witnessed a holism to 'being saved' – for, make no bones about it, the energy that generated this vision came from a deep conviction that God's liberating reign makes possible not only individual salvation, but the peace of the neighbourhood and the city. 'Because,' says Gornik, 'the *charis* of New Song places the church at the heart, if this is compromised, so is the entire project. A healthy neighbourhood body centred in its calling to seek the peace of the community and city is, in spiritual, sociological and historical terms, crucial for the integrity of mission.'

Redistribution

I have that slightly English scepticism about success stories, but even to my questioning spirit, New Song has been a phenomenal success. Much of its vision has been articulated by three or four people. Mark's skill in raising money, creating business partnerships, and in keeping the focus 'rooted in the lives of the broken-hearted', has been essential to the achievements thus far. In the same way Alan and Susan Tibbells, together with Laverne Stokes, have anchored many of the projects, ensuring their ongoing viability.

At heart these visionaries saw the issue of *redistribution* as essential in order for places like Sandtown to have any significant future. By modelling in some small way the biblical vision of justice for the poor, they have demonstrated how Christians can be stewards of God's world and gifts, working for just relationships, especially through the sharing of resources, time and talents. Gornik and his colleagues made partnerships with businesses, churches and local government across the city. These institutions, which provided resources in terms of money and people for all the New Song projects, were themselves evidence of re-born attitudes.

The vision of resurrection exemplified through New Song became a microcosm of the biblical hope *shalom*, often translated as 'peace'. Pinchas Lapide describes this concept of peace, of 'welfare and salvation, well-being, peace of mind, good fortune, and social harmony [as] mutually complementary components of one and the same shalom, itself as indivisible as the biblical oneness of politics, society, nature and theology – all parts of a single world order under the one Creator God.'[8] This 'big picture' of biblical justice is what New Song is seeking to make effective on Sandtown's mean streets.

In this community, as elsewhere, I was interested to observe the effects of September 11. Here for the first time I met face to face with people who, while being personally shocked at the events themselves, nevertheless remarked, 'Every year we see hundreds killed in our neighbourhood. Nobody seems concerned about that. No one raises money or goes to war for us.' A conservative estimate put deaths in the streets over ten years at 3,000. People perceived government as uncaring and discriminatory, and its refusal to share the economic prosperity through programmes of urban renewal as indicators of this malaise.

New Song models a 'church that is *of* and *with* the community, not simply *in* it or *for* it. God's concern for the community is defined by God's love for the hundredth one.' Or put another way, God's concern is for the 'least', or the 'little ones', as Luke's Gospel frequently puts it, or even – as one particularly dramatic translation observes – 'those who cringe'.[9] Such people, and there are many in Sandtown and surrounding neighbourhoods, know all too well the experience of abandonment and they recognise, as do the poor everywhere, that when recession hits they are the first and most critically affected by economic downturn.

The *charis* of New Song holds the wider vision of God's reign or kingdom, which 'is for all of life including housing, health, education and economic development.' When the church's mission takes effect, as it has here, it enters into the realm of 'true liberation'. As Gornik observes of New Song's *charis*, 'liberation – salvation is for all of life, and the ministry of Jesus that sets captives free is central for the church's mission. The church is to celebrate not denigrate God's liberating activity in the neighbourhood.'

This understanding of the reign of God has led to a 'holistic evangelism'. This means a conversion that affects not only individuals, but seeks to transform structures and powers that control human lives, so that it becomes possible for such people 'that we may be able to live peaceful and quiet lives.'[10]

The fourth 'R' – Repentance

Perkins' '3Rs' of *Relocation, Reconciliation* and *Redistribution* have been key to the development of New Song in Sandtown, and more recently in Harlem, New York.[11] In each location the pursuit of *shalom* has been marked by what Lapide calls the

> theo-politics of small steps: [such as] curtailing conflicts, blunting confrontations, waiving rights, keeping and going beyond the law of love, being flexible, and all the thousand and one ways of persistent "busy bee" labour for the "sake of peace" . . . This is to be a human collaboration in the plan of salvation, whose goal remains not merely an absence of conflict, but the full being-at-peace of the world under God.[12]

Addressing this, Gornik and Tibbells believed that a fourth 'R' was essential to their witness in the neighbourhoods – *Repentance.* The model of repentance they spoke of was not so much that of 'feeling' or 'being sorry', but rather being open to a new world view, a sort of putting an end to 'business as usual'.

Referring to the image in John 9 of the man born blind, Gornik reflected:

> Because God had 'spit on our eyes' we believed that we had to deal with the unresolved habits of America's original sin, racism, and to wake up to the tragedy present in our own city. Because of the gospel we could no longer remain 'innocent bystanders,' standing aside as the suffering of Baltimore deepened. Our Christian conversion required us to take specific steps, unlearning old ways of living, and putting on new modes of human existence.

It was this 'waking up', 'unlearning' and 'putting on' of new models of practice, that signified this new repentance.

> God moves us forward to a new way of obedience, a turning in a different direction. For us this has meant taking the pain and the brokenness and racial oppression to be our responsibility, the history of Baltimore and Harlem to be our common history, and therefore a call to repentance.

The events of September 11 provided the world with a new concept -'Ground Zero'. Over the years, on an equally massive scale, the dislocation and de-humanising reality for all too many of the world's poor and marginalised, even those in prosperous nations and major cities like Baltimore, has created a sense of hopelessness and despair. In such places of devastation, death, despair and a sense of no future, New Song had provided a kind of 'wake up call' to the churches, businesses and government, by offering a genuine sign of hope, the possibility of the resurrection or re-birth, not only of individuals, but of whole communities of crucified humanity.

As I prepared to make my pilgrimage to Ground Zero, it began to dawn on me that perhaps the defining 'Ground Zero' moment was on the gibbets of Calvary. I recalled too that if 'the only reason there is Christianity is because of resurrection', then New Song was a sign of it. I recalled the words of Elder Harris at the end of a gathering for celebration one Sunday in Sandtown: 'And now church begins after we leave here; dispersing for the work of doing justice on Monday.'

11

'Ground Zero'

On journeys like this one, where I find myself having to deal with difficult and complex issues, I usually make my way to art galleries. Here I discover two things, both the intellectual and emotional stimulation of looking at an artist's work, and a place of spiritual reflection, opening my soul to see God and humanity in new ways. This period of sabbatical had provided me with a feast of opportunities for my soul.

I had travelled up to Boston to spend Thanksgiving with an old friend Iain and his family. I had spent the following day once again in the Museum of Fine Art; here I had indulged in my passion for the American painters Homer and Sergeant, and lesser-known folks like Thomas Worthington Whittredge, whose painting 'Old Homestead by the Sea' captivated me that day. Here too were impressionists Corot and Millet. As I gazed at Millet's rendering of Irish peasant life in 'The Sower' and the 'Potato Planters', I mused along with him on the question, 'Why should the work of a potato planter be any less interesting or less noble than any other activity?'

The next day Iain and I made our way up to Rockland in Maine to visit the Wyeth Center, where I could view some of my beloved Andrew Wyeth paintings. What captivated me about his style was summed up in his own words: 'If somehow I can, before I leave this earth, combine my absolutely mad freedom and excitement with truth, then I will have done something.'

We were excited at the prospect of our day. Like me, Iain is an admirer of Wyeth, and as we entered the gallery we were confronted with Wyeth's latest work, painted now in his ninetieth year. Strong and bold, it depicted, unlike much of his earlier work, a woman whose face was hidden in a mass of silver white hair. The figure stood on a rock against the backdrop of a storm-tossed sea. For me it carried a sort of finality, and yet a hope. Here it seemed was someone who had found a certain 'absolutely mad' freedom. Foolishly, I did not record its title, but as I recall the painting, I have found myself describing it as 'Wyeth's *resurrection* picture'.

'I think one's art goes as deep as one's love goes'

Our day in Rockland, and along the Maine coast where Wyeth did much of his work, concluded with a visit to a farm on the shore of a rocky cove, a place called Olson's House. Here Wyeth painted his perhaps most famous work, 'Christina's World', which hangs in the Museum of Modern Art in New York. Christina Olson was partially paralysed, and the picture of her making her way up the hillside from the cove to her house depicts both despair and hope.

As we journeyed home we reflected together on our own lives in the light of Wyeth's observation on his. For me the Christian faith is in some senses the marrying of 'my absolutely mad freedom and excitement with truth'. As we had observed the paintings that day, and were later to compound this treat by being taken by another friend, Canon Mark Harris, to Brandywine in Pennsylvania to see an even larger collection of Andrew Wyeth's work, including some permanent exhibits of Helga (see p. 00), I found once again the liberation I had found in Washington those years before. Here was a clarity, an attempt to describe in perfect representation not only an outward observation, but a subject loved. 'I think,' remarked Wyeth on one occasion, 'one's art goes as deep as one's love goes.'

For many years I have tried to paint, and one of the efforts of mine that has given me most satisfaction is an attempt at a copy of Wyeth's 'Loden Coat'. Of course I give too little time to painting, and as Charlie Schultz, creator of *Peanuts,* has Lucy and Linus observe after a visit to an art gallery: 'I learned a lot at the art museum,' says Lucy. 'I did too,' responds Linus. 'I think I learned something very important . . . I'll never be Andrew Wyeth.' Well, I know I won't, but during my few weeks' sojourn in Ireland, I began to understand why I do not find the process of painting satisfying. Simply, I do not love what I set out to paint. If I am to become an artist, it is that love which I have to nurture.

The reason I find my faith so exciting and enjoy its freedom is that over the years I have come to find a profound and deep love for the truth as I see it revealed in the person of Jesus Christ. I have struggled with the individualism of faith with which much modern Christianity is so beset. I believe that somehow or another the crisis with which the world has been confronted since September 11, 2001 provided a unique opportunity for a re-entering into the understanding that Jesus had of a world into which God's kingdom comes, and God's will is done. God's intervention in human affairs is born out of a deep and passionate love for what has been created. God seems to me to invite us to discover that love, receive it, and nurture it not only for God, but also for our fellow human beings and the planet that is given us as gift.

'There is no progress without struggle . . .'

'Tries hard but is handicapped', read my art teacher's terse remark on my first secondary school report. Re-interpreting our faith for these times does not come easily, nor without struggle, because however hard we try we are handicapped by an innate selfishness and self-interest that tends to exclude the 'other' rather than include.

Part of the modern malaise is the ease with which even the most horrific of events so quickly lose their power to change us more than a little. Walking around the neighbourhood where I stayed up on the west side of Central Park, I passed a large housing project dedicated to the name of Frederick Douglass, one of the great black American shakers and movers, who observed, 'There is no progress without struggle.' What he and thousands of his fellow African Americans understood was that there are times in human affairs when things have become so bad that the only solution is a giving up of self in all its forms, and working together for a new and better way. Just how hard it is to acquire justice and the full humanity for which we were created is all too evident for many African Americans today. Intuitively I sense that if '9–11' is not just to be another atrocity in history, we must enter into a period of struggle to re-establish faith in the earth.

Mark Gornik had often spoken to me about the influence that the African American artist Jacob Lawrence (1917–2000) has upon his life. A few days before we visited Ground Zero, Mark took me along to a retrospective exhibition of Lawrence's work at the Whitney Gallery in New York. Through the medium of narrative art Lawrence sought to tell the struggle of African Americans from the days of the Great Migration, which began in the 1920s from the segregated southern states. There is an almost naïve quality about Lawrence's art. His pictures graphically tell 'about trains and people walking to stations . . . field hands leaving their farms to become factory workers, and about families that sometimes got left behind.' He reflected that 'the choices made were hard ones, so I wanted to show what made the people get on those northbound trains. I also wanted to show what it cost to ride them. Uprooting yourself from one way of life to make your way in another involves conflict and struggle. But out of the struggle comes a kind of power, and even beauty.'[1]

Mark and I discussed the ongoing struggles in Harlem and the relevance of this exhibition. Lawrence lived here from the age of thirteen, and today New Song now struggles with issues of gentrification and the making of yet further emigrations by those too poor to stay living in the area. The events of '9–11' have impacted upon the lives of the poor, low-paid workers who live here. The janitors, cleaners, and thousands in menial ancillary jobs have become 'double victims', without work or income and, because of all this, their homes. For while no cause can justify the attacks of that day, as my friend Jim Wallis observed at a meeting we had earlier that week, 'it is impossible to comprehend adequately the terrorist attack of September 11 without a deeper understanding of the grievances and injustices felt by millions of people around the world. [As with segregation and racism over many decades] . . . [that] is a painful subject that the US government refuses to engage, the mainstream media avoids, and many Americans are unable to hear at this moment of mourning, grief and anger.'[2]

Jacob Lawrence's narrative art tells the story of the African American people's 'strength and courage. I share it now,' he writes, 'as my parents told it to me, because their struggles and triumphs ring true today. People all over the world are still on the move, trying to build better lives for themselves and for their families.'[3] The daily litany of the stories of asylum seekers, of enforced emigration throughout the great continents, human beings under God, created and loved by God, seeking to find at some level the humanity given them by God as a birthright.

It seems to me that this requires of people like me, for whom so little has been costly, a listening, a change of heart, a willingness to step into conflict and struggle on behalf of others. As I was writing this I came across some words from the Bishop of Winchester in his 2001 Christmas sermon: 'Would we be in this situation,' he asked, 'if western – north American and European – electorates, all with deep Christian pedigrees, had not encouraged, supported or at least allowed our governments over so many decades to develop our standard of living at the expense of millions in the southern hemisphere? And if we had not sold their rulers armaments on such favourable terms and with so little forethought?' He concludes, 'Cruelly evil though they were, I find that I have to understand the events of September 11th as a judgment upon us; and . . . an opportunity for a fresh beginning, its character caught in these words: "Let the same mind be in you that was in Christ Jesus." '[4]

Ground Zero

It was on one of those stunningly beautiful autumn days that I became conscious of Ground Zero for the first time. We had driven up into the Shawangunk Mountains to visit Minnewaska State Park. Motoring up the Hudson Valley in the brilliant morning sunshine we left the remnants of what must have been a beautiful fall on the outskirts of New York City. The leaf-stripped trees stood silhouetted against a brilliant blue sky. Minnewaska, when we reached it, was a high lake surrounded by impressive cliffs and forests. The day, though cool, was pleasant enough for walking lightly clad. The Gorniks' young son, Peter, clasped my hands as I carried him shoulder high for part of our walk.

Under a brilliant blue sky we sat on the cliff top and recalled how on a similarly beautiful day a few short hours from here came the terror that created what is known now as 'Ground Zero'. Although by the time we were driving home in the late afternoon sun I had been in New York for several days, my arrival in the dark, together with the location of the apartment in which I was staying, meant that I had not seen the Manhattan skyline. As we joined the returning holiday traffic along Route 87, the sunset was spectacular, a kaleidoscope of reds, yellows, greens, blues and black. As we crossed the Hudson, I could see for the first time in the distance the outline of the remaining skyscrapers on the near horizon. The absence of the World Trade Towers struck me for the first time. Here during our last visit with two of our sons, Patrick and John, we had posed for photographs against the backdrop of a sunset not dissimilar from the one we had just witnessed.

One tastes and smells Ground Zero long before reaching the railings and hoardings festooned with prayers, messages, flags and pictures. Like September 11, the morning of our pilgrimage proffered a clear blue, cloudless sky. Mark, Dee and I were welcomed to St Paul's Church by the Rector, Lyndon Harris. This was the church in which George Washington prayed after his inauguration as President. It stood within the shadow of the World Trade Center, yet miraculously escaped without even a window broken. Since '9–11' it has been a place where rescue workers have been ministered to by an endless stream of volunteers who provided food, first aid, massage, as well as space for rest during the long shifts. Around the walls and on the pews of the church itself were hundreds of messages of support and sympathy for the rescuers, as well as for their colleagues who have died in the rescue effort. 'I came here,' said Lyndon, 'to find a ministry. Little did I suspect what kind of ministry, nor its significance.'

We walked out into the graveyard of the church that backed on to the perimeter of the Ground Zero site. A few yards from the boundary fence an excavator tore unremittingly at the pile of rubble, still several stories high. In the background a large crane with a demolition ball which was repeatedly bashed into the stubborn framework of the remains of World Trade Center 7, one of the lesser buildings that formed part of the overall complex. The sheer scale of the site was awesome.

Here we paused and prayed. We began with words from the prayer that had been made during my retreat, offering it for the peace of the world.[5] Then we remembered in particular all from the Diocese of Southwark in South London who had died. We prayed especially for those whose names had been given to me by relatives and friends. As the crane continued demolishing the remains of the building that had become a grave for so many, our voices strengthened as together we prayed 'Our Father . . . your kingdom come . . . forgive . . . as we forgive . . . do not bring us to the time of trial . . .'

Returning to the church, we were accompanied deeper into Ground Zero. We crossed the 'Do Not Cross' police lines equipped with hard hats. Here we were accompanied by a police officer whose soul-destroying task in the weeks since the tragedy was to log and supervise appropriate care for the human remains found on the site. Today it was a woman's hand, which when opened revealed the hand of a baby; and for a few seconds I pictured myself carrying Mark's young son up in the mountains earlier in the week.

We made our way to Fire Station 10. From here the first rescuers ventured into the conflagration of the falling buildings: six of them sacrificed their lives in the early moments of the unfolding cataclysm. At the invitation of the station officer we climbed the stairs to the roof, passing the dust-filled passages and wrecked rooms that once serviced a whole rescue base. A group of firefighters were gathered, tired drawn faces, earnestly searching in the eyes of visitors for signs of hope. For a few moments we shared condolences, thanked them for their tireless work, and offered the continued support of our prayers and thoughts. It felt quite formal, and I thought that once we had 'said our bit' they would drift away. However, we found ourselves caught up in many quiet, earnest conversations, firemen sharing their stories of colleagues, their fears and anxieties. Many were now dispersed around the city; others, too traumatised to work, nevertheless came here for solidarity and companionship.

As we moved to leave the site, we paused and once again offered prayers, now as much for the living as the dead and their relatives. Here amidst the brokenness of buildings we had witnessed the brokenness of lives, and people being asked to bear more than seems humanly possible. It may be somewhat trivial to say that I was looking for signs of hope here, but I was.

At first I found it in the apparently absurd. On the roof of Station 10 that morning was the wealthy socialite Ivana Trump, almost in contradiction, doing a photo shoot for *Hello* magazine. She was offering her support to rebuild the rescue base. I found it, too, in the police officer whose fortitude and determination, cheerful countenance, sympathetic concern and reverence for all human remains, were surely tangible signs of hope. Here in the midst of broken and traumatised human beings, he offered the following reflection: 'This is my life at the moment. Pray for me.' We promised, embraced him and left him to yet another call from somewhere deep within Ground Zero.

Back in St Paul's a eucharist was taking place amidst the comings and goings of the rescue crews. A few used precious moments to receive the gifts of bread and wine, while other colleagues snatched brief periods of rest, a little massage, or a cup of coffee. I was reminded again of how the eucharist celebrates Jesus' resurrection as much as his life and death. To live in a world in which 'my absolutely mad freedom and excitement with the truth' becomes possible for all, and not just a privileged few, I felt a fresh urgency to grasp resurrection not simply as an eschatological hope, but as incarnational possibility, now. I found myself renewed in my desire to practise justice, peace and equality in my own life.

The shocking image of the mother's hand clutching that of a child stayed with me. These fragmentary remains of two 'fearfully and wonderfully made' human beings symbolised more than any words the dehumanising power of violence, oppression and loss in our world. Here in stark awfulness was an icon of broken humanity. In the breaking of the bread, I am reminded that the Christian community drinks the cup 'for the forgiveness of sins', and thereby pledges itself to action for hope; a refusal to repeat mistakes; a choice to live with compassion, forgiveness and understanding; a determination to make a stand against domination by whomever – and to seek the welfare of all.

As we left the church, outside on the railings a constant stream of people were adding mementoes, a name, a flower, a flag, or banner. Tears remained commonplace, and despite the crowds on the sidewalk no one hustled against the background noise of heavy trucks and emergency sirens.

Returning to Mark and Rita's apartment we found a message from London. A few days before, in his address on 29 November, the Archbishop of Canterbury spoke in Westminster Abbey to the families and friends of those United Kingdom citizens who had lost their lives here. He recalled the words of St Paul, 'Nothing can separate us from the love of God', and reflected, 'God's love is the reality that awaits us even when "tower and temple fall to dust." ' And I found myself reflecting that if, as Wyeth observed, 'one's art goes as deep as one's love goes', could I with hope and confidence say, 'one's faith goes as deep as one's love goes' – for God, for humanity, and for the world?

12

'A living hope, from the past into the present, for the future'

'Our passion,' she said, 'is the presence of God in us, in our story. When for any reason we give up on ourselves, we fragment the passion.' I was visiting Sister Grace Myerjack, a contemplative sister of the Maryknoll order whose mother house is at Ossining, a few miles up the Hudson River from New York. Sister Grace and I had been talking about a mutual friend, sharing something of the frustrations he was facing, and reflecting a little on our own faith journeys. For over thirty years Grace has led a contemplative life, and yet her grasp on contemporary affairs and the human condition has led many like me to beat a pathway to her door. There is hope in the past and the present, as well as the future, we had reflected together.

My visits to Maryknoll over a number of years have been times of refreshment, renewal, and frequently challenge. On my first visit here more than ten years ago I had walked in the graveyard overlooking the Hudson valley which marks the last resting place of members of the community. I had marvelled how few folk were buried there, but like most missionary orders, many members had died in lands far from here, some in identified, but many in unknown graves.

I had been greeted as so often in the past by my old friend, Father Jack Halbert, formerly head of the Maryknoll School of Theology. On my first visit in 1991, despite elaborate preparations I was somehow unexpected as a guest. I heard a voice say, 'Who the hell is Peter Price?' 'I am,' I replied as Jack rounded the corner, and we have been friends ever since. Jack had witnessed much of the brutality of the civil war in El Salvador, where he had been a missioner for many years. A tough old bird, he nevertheless reveals one of the warmest and most human beings it has ever been my privilege to meet.

With my sabbatical coming to an end, I sought not only some spiritual guidance here, but also some plain old-fashioned fellowship from people who know how to have a good time, as well as to face the problems of the world with courage and fortitude. Jack's experience on the front line during the 'dirty war' in El Salvador provided him with more insight than most into the world's affairs. For both Jack and Grace, the presence of God in them and in their story provided ongoing evidence of people who had refused for any 'reason to give up on [them] selves' and thus had not fragmented their passion for God, justice and a longing for a new world, despite having faced much of the worst of the pain that the world can throw around.

'Is this your room, or do you share it with someone else?'

A couple of days later Dee and I wandered down to the Lower East Side of Manhattan. Over the years of travel, it has been our privilege to walk in some of the poorest neighbourhoods in the world, often to the dis-ease of our hosts who have feared for our safety, as indeed would we, charged with the responsibility of caring for our guests. Only once have we experienced real hostility, and that was at the tail end of a hurricane during a visit to St Vincent in the Caribbean, when we had walked along the shoreline as boats and houses were being smashed by the wind and waves.

We had gone to the Lower East Side, for here encapsulated in a few streets lies the history of immigration into America. In an area known as Delancey countless millions of immigrants settled where once in the seventeenth century Dutch planters farmed. In the mid nineteenth century, when European immigration was at its peak, opportunistic landowners built the first tenements to house the 'tired, poor, huddled masses yearning to be free', as the plaque on the Statue of Liberty declares. Here between 1845 and 1860 came Irish escaping from the Potato Famine, Germans from civil war, and from 1880 to 1924 Hungarians, Italians, Russians and Eastern European Jews. Following the Second World War came Puerto Ricans, Dominicans, Haitians, Asians, and Bangladeshis.

Preserved in Orchard Street is one such tenement house, now owned by the East Side Tenement Museum Trust. Vacant since 1935, the building with its twenty tiny apartments, 'was as though people had just picked up and left', the museum's curator, Anna Jacobson recalls. 'It was like a little time capsule.' A small group of enthusiasts were determined to preserve 'the stories of the Lower East Side Immigrants and migrants, long overlooked and in danger of being forgotten.'[1]

' "Is this your room, or do you share it with somebody else?" a teenaged boy asks 14–year-old Victoria Confino, as he surveys the 137 square foot space. "I share it with a lot of somebody elses," she says. "I have five brothers." The boy and his classmates have stepped back in time to 1916 to visit Victoria (played by an adult interpreter), who lived with her family at 97 Orchard Street between Broome and Delancey Streets'[2] on New York's Lower East Side.

Victoria Confino was describing a particular moment in the history of this tenement house built in 1863 and occupied continuously until 1935 by thousands of immigrants to the United States. However, within this same house, and throughout this neighbourhood, once the most densely populated district on earth, this 'room' was shared by German, Irish, Eastern European and Chinese immigrants as well as African Americans, who had formerly been slaves.

The Museum's founder, Ruth Abram, speaks of its purpose to reveal that 'behind every door (in this neighbourhood) is a family with a different religion, a different language, each special and unique. But in the hallways, stoops, and streets, all these people are together pursuing the American Dream.'[3] Our visit seemed timely, not least because of our experience at Ground Zero, but also because of the growing fearfulness of many citizens from the Indian subcontinent, even Asia, it seemed an appropriate place to make pilgrimage and offer solidarity. As we listened to our guide describing the multi-ethnic nature of the streets around Delancey, and we thought of the morning's newspaper headlines of beatings being meted out to Muslims, particularly taxi drivers, the words of Kofi Annan on receiving the Nobel Peace Prize in 2001 – 'we see better and we see further . . . that humanity is indivisible' – seemed particularly poignant.

We felt too that Victoria Confino sharing her room with 'lots of somebody elses' was a parable for our planet. The concept of liberty, of a nation composed of immigrants living in harmony, is surely the stuff of Jesus Christ's dream of the 'kingdom come on earth as it is in heaven.' In the story of the tenements we re-discerned Grace Myerjack's words that our passion 'is the presence of God in us, in our story.' For how many has our world become a place where people have given up on themselves and 'fragmented the passion'?

'Imagine all the people . . . living in peace'

As we made our way home that day we walked through Strawberry Fields in Central Park. Following the assassination of John Lennon in New York, a memorial garden had been built in the park in his memory by his widow Yoko Ono and named after the famous Beatles' song 'Strawberry Fields Forever'. Earlier that week George Harrison, another member of the group, had died of cancer and many people had gathered that evening at the memorial garden. As we approached the hidden corner of the park we found ourselves among people who had lit candles, written slogans, eulogies and even prayers. A few ageing hippies smoked pot, and everywhere makeshift memorials were made to Harrison's contribution to world peace. On Lennon's memorial is inscribed the word 'Imagine'. The words of his song of that name ask the listener to 'Imagine all the people of the world living in peace'.

I could not help but reflect that these two 'beat' musicians were drawing a higher profile for peacemaking than anyone else. Disappointment gripped me, for much as I appreciated the music of the Beatles, and found many of their songs enjoyable, and even inspirational, I found almost nihilism in Lennon's world view. He longed for a world in which nations and possessions cease to exist, and through lack of greed, hunger or want, are replaced by sharing. Enviable enough, it was nevertheless a value free world, for here there is 'no heaven', 'no religion', no tomorrow, only 'people living for today'. Somehow it wasn't enough for me.

Biblical reflection and solitude over the past few weeks had been severely limited by the rather public room that Dee and I now occupied back at Mark and Rita's. The teaching of Jesus about being peacemakers, about 'taking no anxious thought for tomorrow', was very much in my mind, as 'the war against terrorism' being promoted was one that was intended to 'last for years and years'. The temptation to bury one's head in pietism had never been greater.

Yet I sensed that part of humanity's yearning was expressed to me on the evening I returned to New York from Boston after Thanksgiving. I sat beside a young woman student, whose array of protest badges, nose and ear-rings had caught my eye as I took my seat beside her. Her name was Eleanor, and she was a student of ethnicity and racism. She also described herself as a 'peace activist'. I asked her what that meant for her. She spoke of how she and a few friends were keeping a diary of news stories and government statements since September 11. 'We are recording truths, half truths and general misinformation,' she said enthusiastically. Peace protests, she admitted, had been difficult, even inappropriate, but educating for peace she saw as an activity that was integral not only to her studies, but to how 'we make the world a different place.'

I was genuinely touched, moved by her zeal, and yet her cool strategy. I shared some of my own adventures in peacemaking. I spoke of my conviction that Jesus Christ sought to bring peace through reconciliation, and that for me the struggle was about how to nurture strategies of conflict resolution, in the Church, in the community, in the world. I shared my conviction that forgiveness, loving, and allowing oneself to receive God's Spirit, seem integral to making true peace.

How often I have found these occasional meetings on trains,

planes and buses to offer 'little friendships' and a sort of meeting with angels, those anonymous messengers of God who seem to both encourage and warn at the same time. Always there is within them a potential for new companionship, an awareness of others 'on the way' to something better, more hopeful, more human, and yes, more divine too.

The dying days of our precious time away included visits to two groups of friends in places about as diverse as it is possible to imagine. We took time out with Jim and Joy Wallis in Columbia Heights, Washington, and with Iain and Riita Liissa Aitken up in Stockbridge, Massachusetts. In surprising ways, the two locations provided extraordinary complementarity.

Facing the reality of a violent world

Jim Wallis, editor of *Sojourners* magazine for over thirty years and the most prophetic voice in faith, politics and culture currently addressing the concerns of our post September 11 world, has been a friend for much of that time.

Early on in my visit we had met in New York, where he had been addressing the question of fundamentalism with the writer Karen Armstrong, the Jewish lawyer-historian Susannah Herschel, and Feisal Abdul Rauf, imam of the al Farah Mosque in New York City and founder of the American Sufi Association. After the debate we repaired to a Hungarian cake shop across from St John the Divine Cathedral, for ongoing discussion around the vexed question of evil, and the gathering war.

In Jim and Joy's home in Washington we continued to 'chew the fat' on this topic. Jim, no stranger to criticising the evils of his own society, with its disregard for the poor, incipient racism, and its military and economical exploitation of much of the 'two-thirds world', nevertheless saw the motivation for the attacks on the twin towers as equally motivated by evil. Committed peacemakers, we were both exercised over the issue of realism in the face of the law of violence that undergirds capitalism, where not only 'the best man wins', but must be seen to win.

We acknowledged our own failure and that of the Church to teach non-violence. We faced together the criticism from fellow travellers who saw in the violence perpetrated on September 11 some measure of divine retribution. We did not feel this was ground that we could safely stand upon, and yet our commitment to peacemaking as integral to the gospel was facing us with particularly difficult challenges.

Earlier that week we had both held separate conversations with our mutual friend Walter Wink[4] about the 'myth of redemptive violence', which he sees as undergirding all justification of modern warfare: that somehow waging war against terrorism by force of arms is ultimately redemptive. Wink repudiates this, arguing that history does not bear out that victory equals redemption; it simply means conquest. Violence ultimately cannot save us. Nevertheless, Wink honestly admitted in his conversation with me and one recorded with Wallis 'to being glad when the "bad guys" lose . . . and women among others are liberated from Taliban tyranny.' Like me, he would prefer that the course of international law and a global policing role could be the means by which conflict is resolved. But he, like Wallis and myself, concluded that at least in part there simply has not been sufficient theology and practice of non-violence taught in our churches.

The need for us as Christians to be realistic weighed heavily upon us in our conversation. In my mind somewhere lay the thought from Jacques Ellul that 'Realism, as generally understood, leads to the conclusion that "things being as they are, this is the realistic line to take." ' But as Ellul continues, 'The Christian must indeed see things as they are, but will not derive his principles of action from them.'[5] As T.S. Eliot has it in 'Burnt Norton', 'humankind cannot bear very much reality'. This is no less true for Christians than for others. The biggest temptation that I have found myself facing in recent days has been a refusal to recognise the facts as they are, and what the immediate future and consequences are likely to be.

In modern parlance such a refusal might be described as denial. It is certainly easier to place one's head firmly in the sand in the mistaken belief that the reality, in this case of retaliation for an act of violation upon the sovereignty of a nation with the power and prestige of the United States, would not happen. It would and it has. Increasingly, the problem for those of us who believe in non-violence and see peacemaking as the core of the faith agenda, is what would be an appropriate response?

Struggling to find a voice

A few days earlier, Jim had been in conversation with Stanley Hauerwas, author of *The Peaceable Kingdom*.[6] He spoke to some extent for us all at the time: 'I just don't feel like I've found a voice about all this yet, but I don't like it when people tell pacifists to just shut up and sit down.' Wallis reflected Hauerwas 'believes that pacifists cannot be expected to have easy policy answers for very difficult political situations that are often created, in part, by not listening to the voices of nonviolence in the first place.'[7]

By the same token, a demand that Christians face reality means that those who advocate non-violence have an obligation to offer alternatives. Sitting in Washington in early December, while the bombs rained down in Afghanistan, demanded some response. I personally do not believe that definitions of 'just war' fit in the modern world. Nevertheless, can one argue that governments that believe retaliatory violence is 'just war' can still be called upon to observe the principle of soldiers killing each other as morally preferable to soldiers murdering civilians?

Surely the minimum peacemakers should strive for in circumstances of war is to advocate the defence of the innocent from retaliation, that 'collateral damage' involving the killing of women, children and non-combatants is unacceptable, and that prevention of widening the theatre of conflict becomes an imperative. None of this takes away from the need to find the perpetrators of terror and bring them to justice.

Part of Christian 'realism' lies in the belief, as Hauerwas has put it, that 'the world changed in 33 A.D., not on September 11th. The question is how to narrate what happened on September 11th in the light of what happened in 33 A.D.' In the Christian story, Wallis and I reflected, what happened in 33 AD was not just the death and resurrection of Jesus Christ, but the sending upon the Church and the world the gift of the Holy Spirit.

Jesus' own actions do not seem to have been born out of a mistaken messianic complex, but rather from the conviction that in the process of confronting reality, he and his followers should be 'wise as serpents and innocent as doves'.[8] Jesus spoke in the context of a religious system that believed in sacrifice, the dove being the sacrifice of the poor. He nevertheless equated himself with the victim. His wisdom lay in understanding why he took such a stance. I began to wonder whether this was to understand the intervention of the Holy Spirit in our world today.

Once again I found Ellul helpful.

> Faith in the Holy Spirit does not mean that we may act imprudently, close our eyes and refuse to think; rather, it means that we must use our heads and try to see with clarity. True, the Holy Spirit – who is clarity itself – may propel us into the greatest impudence, but then we shall know it.[9]

We are living in times when, as Jesus also put it, 'the children of this world are more astute' than we are.[10] We who would be peacemakers must not only practise humility, as Wallis observed, but also take cognisance of Jesus' instruction, that if we are to build a new world, like an architect, we must sit down and make plans which take into account the cost.

Like most of my encounters, this one with Jim and Joy was rewarding, but all too short. We spent pleasant evenings dining out, and before leaving for our final days took the tourist trolley around Washington, just glimpsing through the White House fence at its famous Christmas tree before yet another security scare brought police to close the area once again.

'Tis the gift to be simple . . .'

Up to this point in our sabbatical journey Dee and I had been quite intense, and it was time for a break, a weekend away. We travelled by Greyhound bus into the New England countryside, and up to Stockbridge in Massachusetts. Here we spent a couple of days with old friends.

Stockbridge is one of those film-set villages of white wooden slatted buildings, wide streets and picturesque, slightly naff gift shops and boutiques. We stayed at the *Red Lion Hotel*, described as 'a seventeenth-century coaching inn'. Its timber structure, wide porches, wood fires and Christmas potpourri decorations made it quite a romantic setting – and to cap it all, it snowed! Here the artist and illustrator of 'all American life', Norman Rockwell, lived and worked. His weekly illustrations for the *Saturday Evening Post* over nearly four decades reflected the people and mood of the nation with boldness, clarity and insight.

We arrived earlier than our friends and wandered along the street, amused to discover the site of Arlo Guthrie's renowned 1960s' anti-Vietnam War song 'Alice's Restaurant'. We entertained ourselves by singing a few bars, and recalled occasions when phrases from it, like 'that was horrible', became part of our family vocabulary whenever someone wanted to describe a particularly good meal!

This is Shaker country, and a few miles away lay the Hancock Shaker village. We travelled there on the Saturday. It was a remarkable place, and our day was consumed by the visit. 'The Shakers' was the name given to the United Society of Believers in Christ's Second Appearing, but because of the ecstatic dancing which marked their early worship, people called them 'Shakers'. Shakers were composed of quite ordinary folk, craftsmen and women, clerks, farmers and the like. They 'gave up' homes, families, and livelihoods, seeking within a community to put into practice what they called 'authentic Christianity'.

What made them so remarkable was that before the emancipation of the slaves, and over one hundred years before women received the right to vote, the Shakers practised not only pacifism and feminism, but a social, economic and spiritual equality which few societies have matched. Never large as a movement, the height of their membership was in 1840, when some 6000 believers lived in nineteen communal villages. Their impact has been enormous.

Despite their size in numbers, the Shakers brought into existence many of the gadgets and tools that the modern world has come to take for granted: circular saws, packet seeds, door catches, and many hundreds more inventions. Their craftsmanship was exemplary, causing Thomas Merton once to reflect, 'the peculiar grace of a Shaker chair is due to the fact that it was made by someone capable of believing that an angel might come and sit on it.'

One of the early philosophers of communism, Frederick Engels, observed of the Shakers that they were 'the first people in America, and actually the world, to create a society on the basis of common property . . . Although their religious views, and especially the prohibition of marriage, frightened many away, they have nevertheless found a following.' Many husbands and wives, together with their families, came to the communities, but once resident lived as 'sisters' and 'brothers', the men and women occupying separate sleeping and working areas. Their dancing, they believed, brought them closer to God, although the initial frenzied dancing lasted only for the first ten years of the Society's existence.

The communities, of course, were subject to exploitation, from thieves who stole their vegetables, as much as to the so-called 'winter Shakers', who arrived without fail in the fall, and left in the spring. 'We plant some for the Shakers,' foundress Mother Ann would say, 'some for the thieves and some for the crows. Thieves and crows have to eat too.' They enjoyed recognition by such people as Daniel Hawthorne and Ralph Waldo Emerson, who saw them as wise, and those who 'have truly learned much wisdom'.

As we looked around the great circular barns where twenty haywains and their accompanying horses could enter at a time, together with the mills, dairies, and workshops, as well as the dormitories and meeting rooms, it became possible to agree with the observation of John Humphrey Noyes: 'It is no more than mere justice to say that we are indebted to the Shakers more than to any or all other social architects of modern times. Their success is solid capital that has upheld all the paper theories and counteracted the failures.'

The Shakers were part of a mass utopian movement prevalent in America in the 1840s and onwards – 'it was the age of the Mormons and Oneidans, the Transcendentalists at Brook Farm, the intellectual communities like New Harmony and the North

American phalanx, and the religious sects like Aurora, Amana, Skaneateles, the Harmony Society, Bishop Hill and Icarians. Out of this multitude of experiments, the Shakers were the oldest, and still seemed the soundest.'[11]

As we made our way back to New York, we reflected together that there was something deeply attractive about the simplicity and egalitarian nature of the Shaker experiment. Perhaps, we considered, it is simplicity that ought to be the watchword of any new world order that is truly to embrace the possibility of peace and justice for all. Like all utopian dreams it foundered, though a few Shakers remain, and there is talk of a revival up in New England. But as an experiment in chosen freedom it is certainly challenging. I simply couldn't get out of my head the famous Shaker tune, which many of us know as 'Lord of the Dance', and the words:

> 'Tis the gift to be simple,
> Tis the gift to be free,
> 'Tis the gift to come down where we ought to be,
> And when we find ourselves in a place called right,
> 'Twil be in the valley of love and delight.
>
> When true simplicity is gained,
> To bow and to bend we shall not be ashamed.
> To turn, turn, turn, will be our delight,
> 'Til by turning, turning,
> We come out right.

Playing the Blue Note – A Postscript

There is in the Irish language a poetry that somehow gives to the ordinary and everyday a new perspective. Many mornings during my five-week 'Lenten' sojourn in Ireland I had witnessed the dawn. Sometimes a bright sun rising through a dark circle of cloud, or the glistening of silver shimmering on a grey sea. In the Irish there is a phrase for the dawn – *Fainne Gheal an Lae.* 'Now *Fainne* is a ring and *Ghael* is "bright" or "silver bright", and *an lae* is "of the day".'[1] For a while I wanted to call this book *Bright Ring of the New Day,* because for me the encounters in it with God, myself, friends, acquaintances, new and old, as well as of saints known and unknown, have offered to my life many new moments of brightness, new dawnings, new hope.

Hoping . . . in spite of the evidence

And hope is a commodity in short supply in our times. I don't mean that many of us are not 'hoping for the best', or desirous of a future that is not marred by bitterness, hatred, conflict and war. Of course we are, but the hope that lifts us into confident belief in God who brings life out of death, and who inspires us to live more complete, wholesome and focused lives, committed to the well-being of others, and a search for universal peace – that is what is missing. Jim Wallis has put the imperative of hope like this: 'Hope is believing, in spite of the evidence, and watching the evidence change.'

When a new Christian in my teens I, together with friends, would regularly take services at our local old people's homes. We were eager to bear witness to our new-found faith in Jesus Christ, and the residents were subject, Sunday by Sunday, to our enthusiasm for their souls! I was reminded of this recently when I passed quite accidentally one such place that I had visited over forty years before. Since then I have had a certain resistance to visiting homes for the elderly. However, during our brief sojourn in Delaware, we were invited by our friend Mark Harris to visit his 84-year-old mother in a nearby residential home.

I confess that my heart sank! All kinds of uncharitable thoughts came to mind – like 'Why, just because Mark is feeling guilty about visiting his mother, do we need to be dragged in to see her?' *Mea culpa*! We entered this beautiful purpose-built village for the mature in years, and eventually into the room of Anne Eldridge Harris.

Anne stood to greet us. Around her on the walls were pictures that she had painted, first in her years as a fine artist, and more recently as one of the world's leading computer generated 'naïve' artists. On a table were stacked a small pile of handbound and printed copies of several of her recent publications, on subjects such as 'growing old', 'bereavement', and a wonderful collection of sayings from various people who had given her hope and inspiration over the years. As we talked, Anne explained that her art was now done using the mouse on the computer. Each day she was on the Internet chatting to other computer fine artists, sharing examples of her work, but also with hospital professors and geriatricians who wanted her insight into the experience of ageing which she had been so articulate in expressing both in word and picture.

Her work was both moving, and amusing. Writing of when her husband died offered both pathos and an insight into loss. Yet within the same book, she has the most wonderful computer-generated picture of herself trying to put on panty-hose – underneath, the caption read 'Putting on pantyhose takes a little longer at my age'. Her practical wisdom, deep faith and sheer love of life both humbled and inspired.

A few nights before, there had been spectacular meteor

showers in the late night sky. Around 2 a.m. she and a neighbour had wrapped themselves in duvets, socks and slippers, sitting out on the tiny balcony in the chill autumn weather, witnessing the event through binoculars. The following day, Anne had recreated the scene on the canvas of her computer screen, and then patiently printed and made cards to celebrate the event.

We were genuinely sorry to leave, yet as we did so, she pressed into Dee's hand a copy of her little book on ageing to give to her 84-year-old Mum – who too is a remarkable woman of hope. Both women, in their own inimitable way, have refused to let life with all its sorrows, as well as its joys, lose that kind of hope that is integral to making the world a place for harmony and wholeness. In the so-called 'twilight years', here was someone who had come to practise 'the gift to be simple, and the gift to be free'.

'Encountering the sacred'

My journey over the past months has led to many 'personal moments of encountering the sacred', often in people, in works of art, through conversations, and in moments of solitude, prayer and reflection. The vigil on the Donegal cliff top, through to the wasteland of Ground Zero, where in the random destruction a large piece of twisted metal formed a cross high over the site, to the 'absolutely mad freedom' of Wyeth's art, and for me his inspirational 'resurrection' picture: each of these had drawn me to a wonderment, a penitence, and a longing. Each had brought me into contact with the Divine, the Holy. In the privilege of solitude and community, I had re-engaged with the God of hope, and found it possible to hope again that the just and gentle rule of God might find root in the earth.

On our last evening in New York, Mark Gornik and I fulfilled both an ambition and a dream by visiting the Blue Note Jazz Club in Greenwich Village. We had arrived early, so as to be able to sit at the tables closest to the artistes performing that evening. The Blue Note is a very intimate venue, and many artistes, unlike those in large concert halls, have a rapport and warmth of relationship with their audiences. That night was no exception. The legendary jazz pianist, Chick Corea, was top of the bill, playing on this occasion with Gonzalo Rubalcara, a Cuban and himself an influential pianist in contemporary jazz.

Jazz is an extraordinary medium. Many who know little or nothing about it do not understand that it is a distinct and demanding musical style based on its own discipline of chords and scales, no less demanding than that of classical music. Listening to these two aficionados of piano jazz that evening, I became conscious of two things: first, how in jazz people need not only to listen to one another, but as Wynton Marsalis the doyen of jazz trumpeters once remarked, 'You have to keep your eyes open – keep your minds open.'[2] In jazz the musician has to improvise, and in the act of improvisation it is hard to maintain the discipline of the original theme. Of course within that improvisation there is huge freedom, but with the freedom there goes hand in hand a need for discipline. The potential for chaos in jazz is ever present, as I sense it is too within my spirituality.

I find myself drawn to jazz as a means of interpreting my own spirituality. My son Patrick is no mean trumpet player; trained classically, he nevertheless plays regularly with some of the best jazz and session musicians around. He talks honestly about the genius of some of these folk, and of how, because of their distinctive training, they are able to achieve both notes and chord structures that are beyond him.

Playing the 'blue note'

Because my own musical skills are limited to a little bit of 'playing by ear' at the piano, I pick up much of what I am learning about jazz music from casual conversations, often with Pat. One of the characteristic features of jazz is that harmonies are enriched by adding notes. What makes jazz distinctive is its capacity for surprise, the creation of the unexpected. This is done, so I am told, by substituting an unexpected chord for a more familiar or common one. The experienced listener to jazz will come to anticipate what might follow, but the genius of the artiste is to make a substitution of a note or chord that takes the hearer by surprise. In jazz, harmonies are enriched by the adding of a single note, nothing apparently complex, but through its imposition creating a unique sound that releases in both the player and the hearer that unique moment of joy.

This journey has been one in which I have experienced something of what it means to 'free that Spirit in which the Redeemer gave his life for us', as John Woolmer, whom I quoted earlier, has it. I have been a witness to elements of the 'new fire' arising from the ashes of cold traditionalism, neglect and despair, whether in the rural environment of south-west Donegal, or the streets of Harlem, Sandtown, or Columbia Heights. In each place, and in countless people, I had discovered that surprise of the adding of the 'note' or 'chord' of hope. But for hope to be true hope, it must arise from taking account of what is the daily reality that for many, if not all of us, at times is cynicism, despair, fear and defeat.

Within the tradition of jazz is that of the 'Blues'. The Blues have become the way in which when something tragic happens, it has to be both expressed and, to quote Marsalis again, 'shaken off'. Because jazz grew out of a fusion between black and white music in the southern states of America, it is a blend of African rhythms and the more western idea of harmony. The Blues themselves are secular and, says Marsalis again, 'give a secular optimism in the face of tragedy' but, he continues, 'there is a religious conception too', a sense of the sacred, 'which is uplifting. For Blues has an element of play about it, it is designed to help you survive a tough condition.'

I like this idea of 'play' of which Marsalis speaks about the Blues. Of course he does not mean that light-hearted, carefree play, but rather the art of learning to look at the often dire circumstances from which the music arises, and to deal with it in such a way that the spirit is lifted, and optimism can be contemplated. Because so much of jazz, Blues and Gospel music are interwoven, it is impossible to separate the influences. So in Gospel music the 'hymns, blues, forms of church music, the "Amen" cadence, is a basic progression of the Blues – as are the shouts, moans, and "Christs" ' that intersperse the Gospel songs. 'Everyone', concludes Marsalis, 'is aware of the church sounds – even if they didn't grow up in the church. Musicians are as important as the ministers.'

Much of this reflection went through my head as I sat transfixed by the playing of Chick Corea in the Blue Note Jazz Club on that December evening in the week before Christmas. The past months had brought encounters with the sacred and the secular, with people of faith, and many of none. I had observed as one and then another had dealt with the tragedy and aftermath of September 11; many with anger, resurgent patriotism, even through a reversal of previously held attitudes of pacifism, now demanding retaliation, if not revenge. I had noticed this as much among my Christian acquaintances as among those who made no profession of faith. I also discovered the opposite in people of faith and of no faith, who nevertheless saw that new understanding of those with different cultures and creeds would be a better way forward than the meting out of yet more death and destruction.

I had discovered something of the truth of Tennessee Williams' observation, that 'time is the longest distance between two places', and my pilgrimage to a sacred centre of hope, even when faced with dire moments of despair, had been profoundly transformative. My conviction that there is resurrection, not only in the future but in the present, had been evidenced in the stories of many whose lives had touched mine, and of whom I have written in these pages. But equally, I am strengthened in my conviction that the space-time moment of the resurrection of Jesus Christ remains the most important moment of history, for it has, to quote James Alison again, 'recast the possibility of the human understanding of God.'

The God whom I have come to discover once again is the Supreme Jazz Musician who creates the note of unexpected joy that releases in us hope, and offers us the future harmony of justice, love and peace.

Notes

An introduction

1. Charlotte Bingham, *The Blue Note* (Bantam Books, 2000).
2. Hebrews 11:1.

***Chapter 1:* 'A three-days' journey into the wilderness'**

1. Maggie O'Kane in BBC Radio 4's *Off the Page.*
2. Phil Cousineau, *The Art of Pilgrimage* (Element Books, 1999).
3. James Alison, *The Joy of Being Wrong – Original Sin in the light of the Resurrection* (Crossroad, 1998).
4. *ibid.*
5. Exodus 5:1.
6. Exodus 5:3.
7. Matthew 3:15.
8. Rudy Wiebe, *The Blue Mountains of China* (McClelland and Stewart, 1970).
9. Wade Clarke Roof, *Spiritual Marketplace: Baby Boomers and the Remaking of American Religion* (Princeton, 2001).
10. Anthony de Mello, *Song of the Bird* (Image, 1984).
11. Bruce H. Lescher, 'Catholicism and Post Modernity,' *The Way*, Vol. 41 (July 2001), no. 3.
12. Peter B. Price, *Undersong: Listening to the Soul* (Darton, Longman and Todd, 2002).

***Chapter 2:* 'One whose gently-holding hands . . .'**

1. Matthew 3:4.
2. Matthew 4:2.
3. Luke 24:35.
4. I obtained this from the *Sojomail* network of *Sojourners* magazine, Washington, DC. I think it may be a prayer of Henri Nouwen.
5. Robert Ellsberg, *All Saints – Daily Reflections on Saints, Prophets and Witnesses for Our Time* (Crossroad, 1997).
6. Rainer Maria Rilke, *Selected Poems* (Picador, 1987).

7. Karl Jenkins, *The Armed Man: A Mass for Peace* (Virgin Records).
8. Isaiah 43:1; Psalm 139:2, 9–10.
9. Hosea 11:4.
10. Psalm 139:10.
11. J. Oswald Sanders, *Problems of Christian Discipleship* (China Inland Mission, 1958).
12. 1 Chronicles 4:10.
13. Paul Tournier, *Meaning of Gifts* (SCM Press, 1964).

***Chapter 3:* 'Pleasing God . . .'**

1. Psalm 104:25, 26, 35.
2. Isaiah 58:5.
3. Isaiah 58:5–12.
4. See my reflections on prayer in *Undersong* (Darton, Longman and Todd, 2002).
5. Barry Lopez, *Crossing Open Ground* (Picador, 1987).
6. Barry Lopez, *About this Life* (Harvill, 1998).
7. Matthew 4:1–11.
8. Mark 1:21–39.
9. Ched Myers, *Binding the Strong Man – A Political Reading of Mark's Story of Jesus* (Orbis, 1988).
10. Mark 8:36.
11. Mark 3:1–6.
12. Vincent Van Gogh, *The Complete Letters of Vincent Van Gogh* (New York Graphic Society, 1959), Vol. 1, p. 197.
13. Michael Ford, *Wounded Prophet – A Portrait of Henri J.M. Nouwen* (Darton, Longman and Todd, 1999).
14. John 4:31.
15. Luke 15:1–10.

***Chapter 4:* 'Freely cease from fighting'**

1. Robert Ellsberg, *All Saints – Daily Reflections on Saints, Prophets and Witnesses for Our Time* (Crossroad, 1997).
2. Matthew 25:31–46.
3. vv. 31–2, emphases mine.
4. Raymond McAfee Brown, *Unexpected News: Reading the Bible with Third World Eyes* (Westminster/John Knox Press, 1984).
5. See 'The Martyrdom of Polycarp' in Cyril C. Richardson (ed.), *Early Christian Martyrs* (Macmillan, 1970).
6. Sr Annita Mazrie Caspary IHM, *Francois Mauriac,* The Christian Critic Series B (Herder, n.d.).
7. Genesis 12:1–4.
8. Genesis 18:1–18.
9. Genesis 17:8.
10. Genesis 19:1–29.

11. Jeremiah 18:1–12.
12. John 3:1–17.
13. Matthew 5:43–8.
14. John 2:13–22.
15. Paul S. Minnear, *John: The Martyr's Gospel* (Pilgrim, 1984).
16. Numbers 21:4–9.
17. Mina C. Klein and H. Arthur Klein, *Kathë Kollwitz: Life in Art* (Schocken, 1975).
18. Danny Collum *et al.*, 'A.J. Muste: Pilgrim for Peace through a Century of Wars', *Sojourners* (December 1984).
19. Robert Bonazzi, *Man in the Mirror: John Howard Griffin and the Story of Black Like Me* (Orbis, 1997).
20. Joan Chittister, *Passion for Life: Fragments of the Face of God* (Orbis, 1996).

***Chapter 5:* 'Watch and pray'**

1. Joan Chittister, *Fire in these Ashes* (Gracewing, 1996).
2. Jacques Ellul, *Prayer and Modern Man* (Seabury Press, 1979).
3. From Eucharistic Prayer 'E', *Common Worship* (Church House Publishing, 2000).
4. Luke 18:8.
5. Matthew 26:41.
6. Matthew 26:41 RSV.
7. Revelation 3:17.
8. Genesis 2:17.
9. Ellul, *Prayer and Modern Man;* Ellul uses the word 'man' for which I have transposed in the interests of inclusivity 'humanity'.
10. Matthew 5:9.
11. 2 Corinthians 5:19.
12. Ellul, *Prayer and Modern Man,* p. 167 (the Scripture passage to which he refers is Luke 14:28–33). During my retreat I have found Jacques Ellul's insights profoundly helpful. His writing is made in a philosophical, questioning style that many modern readers would find distracting, rather than difficult. What he has to say, however, is so profound and important to our understanding of prayer that I wanted some forum for his thinking to find expression, and have risked significant quotation from him for the enrichment of all our praying.
13. 2 Corinthians 5:19.
14. 1 Timothy 2:2.
15. Ellul, *Prayer and Modern Man.*
16. Mark 2:1–12.
17. Revelation 2:17.
18. Dee's birth name is Edith, which means 'rich gift'.
19. Thomas Merton, *Seeds of Contemplation* (Anthony Clarke, 1961).

***Chapter 6:* 'Waging reconciliation'**

1. Radio Telefis Eireann – Irish television.
2. This phrase comes from the Statement from the Bishops of the Episcopal Church of the USA following their meeting on 26 September 2001.
3. Robert Ellsberg, *All Saints – Daily Reflections on Saints, Prophets and Witnesses for Our Time* (Crossroad, 1997).
4. 'On Waging Reconciliation' – a Statement from the Bishops of the Episcopal Church released by the Office of the Presiding Bishop on 26 September 2001: the quotation is from *The Book of Common Prayer* of the Episcopal Church of the United States of America.
5. Colossians 1:20, translation not given.
6. John 4:46–54.
7. John 1:13 JB.
8. John 4:48.
9. John 4:53.
10. John 3:7.
11. David Rensberger, *Overcoming the World: Politics and Community in the Gospel of St John* (SPCK, 1988).
12. John 3:19.

***Chapter 7:* 'It is better to light a candle . . . than to curse the darkness'**

1. This longer phrase was attributed to McDyer, although I have chosen the shorter, better known, 'It is better to light a candle than to curse the darkness' as the title to this chapter.
2. *Fr. McDyer of Glencolumbkille – An Autobiography* (Brandon, 1984).
3. *ibid.*, p. 116.
4. Jonah 3.
5. The source of this quote is from the documentary film script: *The Shakers: Hands to Work, Hearts to God* by Ken Burns, copyright of the Hancock Shaker Village Museum, Massachusetts.
6. The 2001 Nobel Peace Prize was awarded to the United Nations and its Secretary General on 10 December 2001. Editing what I had written earlier, it seemed appropriate to include these observations at this point.

***Chapter 8:* 'I arise today . . . through God's strength to pilot me'**

1. 2 Timothy 2:22–5 NRSV.
2. In his book *Iron John* (Element) Robert Bly quotes these remarks of Jung's. I read them first during a retreat where I was attempting to address issues around anger, disappointment and ambition.
3. Elisabeth O'Connor in a private conversation with me in Washington, DC.
4. The story of the transfiguration occurs in Luke 9:28–36, and Jesus'

healing of the Gerasene demoniac follows immediately afterwards (Luke 8:37–43). His life had been threatened for the first time during his visit to the synagogue in Nazareth recorded in Luke 4:18–30.

5. Luke 4:8.
6. Luke 9:35.
7. 1 Kings 19:11ff.
8. Exodus 19 records Moses meeting with God; Exodus 20 recounts the commandments for a just nation; Exodus 32 records the act of rebellion, and Exodus 33 and 34 record Moses returning to the mountain.
9. Ephesians 6:10–17.
10. Luke 9:29.
11. Luke 9:22.
12. Clarence Jordan, *The Substance of Faith and Other Cotton Patch Sermons* (Association Press, 1972).
13. This song has been recorded on *The Pilgrim* – composed by Shaun Davey Tara, CD3032.

***Chapter 9:* 'Journeying outwards – and inwards'**

1. Barry Lopez, *Crossing Open Ground* (Picador, 1989).
2. I first came across the use of this term in Noel Dermot O'Donoghue, *The Angels Keep their Ancient Places – Reflections on Celtic Spirituality* (T&T Clark/Continuum, 2001).
3. These and other quotes from Lopez, *Crossing Open Ground.*
4. Gerard Hughes, *In Search of A Way* (Darton, Longman and Todd, 1986); William Least Heat-Moon, *Blue Highways* (Pimlico, 2001).
5. From some exhibition notes at *The Art that is Life* exhibition, Boston Museum of Fine Arts 1987.

***Chapter 10:* A New Song**

1. John Perkins, *With Justice for All* (Ventura Regal Books, 1992).
2. Mark R. Gornik, *To live in Peace* (Eerdmans, 2002).
3. 1 Corinthians 2:1–5.
4. John 9.
5. The term *charis,* which means 'gift', is widely understood in contemporary interpretation as relating in particular to the gifts of the Spirit which individuals may possess. Gornik uses the term to describe the 'unique calling of a church. A church's *charis* is not an individual vision or ecclesiastical type, but a gift of the Spirit. The Spirit calls a *charis* into being, and this is the church's primary relationship. Thus a church's *charis* is a gift from God to be used for God's mission in the world.' These remarks are made in a so far unpublished paper: 'The *Charis* of New Song: Responding to the Gift and Call of the Spirit.'
6. Gornik, *To live in Peace.* Many of my conversations with Gornik led to his using phrases that I occasionally checked against a rough draft

of his book. Some confusion may exist therefore over what is in the final version of Mark's book and our discussion.

7. Acts 2:47 RSV.
8. Pinchas Lapide, *The Sermon on the Mount: Utopia or Program for Action?* (Orbis, 1986).
9. Richard Cassidy, *Jesus, Politics and Society: A Study of Luke's Gospel* (Orbis, 1978).
10. 1 Timothy 2:2.
11. In 1997 Mark and Rita Gornik moved to Harlem to begin a New Song project in a long neglected neighbourhood of New York. Currently Rita, who was one of the early volunteer doctors at the Sandtown New Song Health Center works in the area of Addiction Abuse, while Mark is developing the City Theological Seminary which will focus on developing ministries from African, Hispanic, and Central European Americans.
12. Pinchas Lapide, *op cit.*, p. 35.

***Chapter 11:* 'Ground Zero'**

1. *The Great Migration – An American Story – Paintings by Jacob Lawrence* – The Museum of Modern Art New York (HarperCollins Publishers).
2. *Sojourners* (November/December 2001).
3. *The Great Migration.*
4. Michael Scott-Joynt is Bishop of Winchester, and an edited extract from his Christmas sermon was published in *The Guardian*, 28 December 2001.
5. The prayer can be found on pages 16–17.

***Chapter 12:* 'A living hope, from the past into the present, for the future'**

1. The data and comments on the East End Tenement museum are from *A Tenement Story – The History of 97 Orchard Street and the Lower East Side Tenement Museum* who are also the publishers. Stuart Millier and Sharon Seitz are the co–authors.
2. *ibid.*
3. *ibid.*, p. 10.
4. Walter Wink, a former professor at Auburn Theological Seminary, New York, is the author of several books on redemptive violence and the powers that rule our world, most notably perhaps *Engaging the Powers* (Fortress, 1992).
5. Jacques Ellul, *Violence* (Mowbray, 1978).
6. Stanley Hauerwas, *The Peaceable Kingdom* (University of Notre Dame Press, 1983).
7. Elements of this conversation were recorded in 'Hard Questions for Peacemakers', *Sojourners* (January–February 2002).
8. Matthew 10:16 RSV.

9. Ellul, *Violence,* pp. 82–3.
10. Luke 16:8.
11. This and various other quotes relating to the Shakers are from *The Shakers: Hands to Work, Hearts to God* by Ken Burns, published by the Hancock Shaker Village Museum.

Playing the Blue Note – A Postscript

1. This description comes from Noel Dermot O'Donoghue, *The Angels Keep their Ancient Places* (T&T Clark, 2001).
2. The quotes from Wynton Marsalis in this chapter have come mostly from *Wynton Marsalis – The South Bank Show,* London Weekend Television, broadcast on 19 November 1995. The programme had something of an impact upon me, as I had been reflecting on my parents that day who, had they lived, would have been celebrating their fifty-fifth wedding anniversary.